W9-BUG-273

How to Succeed at Aging

Without Really Dying

LYLA BLAKE WARD

How to Succeed at Aging

Without Really Dying

PUBLISHED BY

amazon encore

PRODUCED BY

Printed in the United States of America

10 11 12 13 14 15 16 / 10 9 8 7 6 5 4 3 2 1

Published by AmazonEncore
P.O. Box 400818
Las Vegas, NV 89140

Produced by Melcher Media, Inc.
124 West 13th Street
New York, NY 10011
www.melcher.com

Library of Congress Control Number
2010902393

ISBN-13: 978-1935597-00-1
ISBN-10: 1-935597-00-0

Jacket design by Ben Gibson
Interior design by Jessi Rymill
Author photo by Chris Rexon Photography

SUSTAINABLE FORESTRY INITIATIVE
Certified Chain of Custody
Promoting Sustainable Forest Management
www.sfiprogram.org

Melcher Media strives to use environmentally responsible suppliers and materials whenever possible in the production of its books. For this book, that includes the use of SFI-certified interior paper stock.

. . .

To my husband, Russ
And my daughters, two,
Gina and Bindy—
This book's for you

. . .

CONTENTS

Who Are You Calling Middle-Aged?

I have never been middle-aged. I almost was, but just as I approached 45 and was resigned to reaching that particular stage of life, the rules changed. Word came down from WICSLSD (Whoever Is in Charge of Setting Life Stage Dates) that newly published actuarial figures lead us to believe 50 is a more realistic time to be considered at the midpoint in one's life.

Okay, I could live with that, and did, until I found out a few days before I turned 50, they moved the goalposts again. A bulletin circulated. Middle age now begins at 55. How could I explain my expanding waistline as middle-age spread when, at 50, my status was still in limbo? All those marathon-running, mountain-climbing, kick-boxing grandmothers had done it again. In fact, their lobby argued, who could really say when middle age began? I could. Enough already. On my 55th birthday, one dress size larger, silver threads streaking wildly through my otherwise dark hair, I thought: if not me, who? I knew a middle-aged woman when I saw one in the mirror. The title was mine.

Close but no cigar. As more Smuckers honorees were

living to a respectable 110 years old, still playing bridge and—heaven help us—driving their Model Ts around town, society was inclined to give a little more leeway to the 60-to-65 crowd. Maybe they were technically middle-aged, but they weren't sporting gold watches—yet. People were retiring later, having second and even third careers, and for all intents and purposes, middle age just went—*poof!* It disappeared.

Result? I was never middle-aged. I went directly from young to old, without passing Go. Did I say old? Sorry about that. I am euphemistically called a "senior," a title I share with 40 million other Americans documented to be over 65.

And that's what this book is about. Living life in a world of bubble packs you can't open, electronics you struggle to understand, and expiration dates you can only hope don't apply to you. It's also about telephone menus, drug advertising, polls and more polls, computers, and the endless advice given to us by the X, Y, Z generations, who are now filling the age slots we so recently vacated. In columns and books, we are bombarded with information on keeping everything from our hair to our gallbladders. We have antiaging creams at our disposal, minerals and vitamins to keep our wheels spinning, and Sudoku to keep those little gray cells working overtime. We know how to succeed at aging without really dying, because we've been told so often how to do it.

But as one who was cheated out of the entitlements of middle age, I'm wary of societal forces that are working so hard to keep me young. In other words, keep your handheld digital fire extinguishers away from my birthday candles. These writings are the way I see things now, while sitting comfortably on my couch, eating popcorn in the middle of the afternoon, and watching movies that were young when I was.

—LBW

ON AGING

I look in the glass,
And lo and behold,
I see that the mirror
Is getting quite old.

How to Succeed at Aging Without Really Dying

I'm a great believer in self-help. I always was. After college, I read every article I could find on "Successful Job Hunting." Then I went on to "How to Have a Successful Marriage," followed by "Successful Parenting," "How to Pay for College," and "Tips for a Successful Retirement."

I soaked up all the advice, and if I do say so myself, I think I was a pretty fair whatever-stage-I-was-at. But now, just when I want to spoon into a hot fudge banana split with whipped cream on top because "I deserve it," or read a book on a quiet afternoon because "It's now my turn," I'm made to feel guilty. The advice givers are at it again. And who's the target? In books, articles, and lectures, the hottest topic of the day is: Successful Aging. It's not enough that I *am* the ripe old age of _____, I have to prove I'm good at it.

Gerontologists, who generally have 40 or more years to go before *they* become geriatric, say if I don't eschew fat, embrace antioxidants, and double up on my ginkgo biloba, I'm just asking for all those health problems associated with the golden years. Under such banners as "Your Later Years Can Be Your Greater Years" or "Don't Be a

Docile Fossil," they say whatever happens to my body is pretty much up to me. If I did the London *Times* crossword puzzles instead of those wimpy *New York Times* fill-ins, I might not forget the name of a movie or a book or my husband. Even those frequent trips to the bathroom are apparently all a question of mind over bladder.

I'm cautioned to "use it or lose it." And I do swim three times a week, which makes me feel pretty good about myself, until I read those stories about 85- or 90-year-olds running the New York Marathon or a woman my age mountain climbing in Tibet. Then I start worrying. Am I living up to my potential? Last week when my neck went out of whack, I didn't swim for two days. I kept asking myself, would any of those other ladies have stayed in her tent just because her neck hurt? A stronger liniment, maybe, but give up? Never.

According to the articles, if I don't get this thing right, I will be letting down my whole family. My daughters will be crushed when they come in and see me watching afternoon soaps for the first time in my life. And how will I feel when I see the unspoken words in their eyes? "How could you?" "You're not even *trying* to be a successful old person."

Still, some of the research the pros cite *is* impressive. We're told birds keep their feathers until the day they die, fish their scales, and deer their fur. And I'll admit, even up close, it's hard to tell a fawn's skin from a doe's skin. From all reports, animal cells, even those of aging animals, are things of beauty. Mine should look so good. But what those guys don't mention is whether a 50-year-old elephant's memory is as good as a 20-year-old's, or whether a 14-year-old cod remembers how his fish tale ends. Does anyone know for sure if oysters get osteoporosis, or if those hyper hares have stronger hearts than those sluggish tortoises? Are bees subject to diabetes? Clearly, all the returns are not yet in.

And personally, I have some nagging doubts based on my own research. Consider the case of my mother-in-law who lived to 95 eating a half pound of M&M's, a pint of Häagen-Dazs coffee ice cream, and Entenmann's butter crumb cake every day of her life. Mention fiber to her, and she would have thought you were talking about hemp. Her reading in her later years was limited to mystery novels, and the closest she ever got to a gym was walking by it on her way to the beauty parlor.

That's not to say I think all health advice is bunk, or that I'm going to stop looking at the expiration dates on my vitamins. But on the topic of Successful Aging, I have this to say to every writer who has written, is writing, or plans to write an article or book telling me how to do it: *chill out*. For better or worse, I want to do it myself!

Target Audience

Oh, to be 18-to-49 again! To count in the ratings, to have advertisers throw their dollars in my direction! Well, not exactly in *my* direction, but in the direction of the networks who throw things in my direction.

If I were in this magic group, I could stand tall knowing I was part of a target audience. A target audience. Do you have any idea the advantages that go along with being a target? First, your every desire is taken into account. If you show signs of wanting autopsies on prime time, *whoosh*, they're yours. Reality programs? You've got them. If you blink in the direction of alien teenagers as seen through the Hubble telescope, Fox will add it to its fall lineup.

Those ad agencies have done their homework. Their research, funded by the Committee to Preserve Youth in Advertising, seems to show that 18-to-49ers are the only ones who buy cereal, detergents, cars, computers, copiers, soda, mortgages, fabric softeners, shampoo, vacations, perfume, paint, soup, deodorants, aspirin, insurance, vitamins. Ergo, want to sell your products? Reach the preboomer crowd, and you've got it made. Or do you? A recent study showed that "older" people watch over three hours of television a day, more than any other age group. Granted, some may be watching from their La-Z-Boy recliners, but, strange to tell, others are watching while jogging on a NordicTrack in the evening, during prime time. And, contrary to common belief, even people over 50 eat cereal (preferably fortified with calcium and 22 supplements), drink soda, and buy cars, to mention a few extravagances of this elderly crowd. And those over 65, the *really* old, are the fastest-growing segment of the population. Has anyone run those statistics up the flagpole recently?

I don't think so, because I would know if, by some stroke of fortune, someone "up there" had said, "Let's make *her* a target now." I would know, because instead of being relegated to watching reruns of *Murder She Wrote*, which I've seen so many times I know who did it before Jessica does, there would be brand-new programs on, programs designed to please me and my friends. I would be getting questionnaires begging *me* to respond and asking *me* what kind of programs *I* like to watch. They might even ask what kind of products *I* buy and if commercials influence *my* decisions.

But that's all pie-in-the-sky stuff (Pepperidge Farm or Mrs. Smith, take your pick). I'm not looking for miracles here, just a few more rings around the bull's-eye. Maybe next fall's TV lineup could include a program or two for 50-year-olds, the next year 51-year-olds, and so on. At least then, the zoomers might be spared the agony of watching reruns of *Friends* for the rest of their natural lives.

Too Many Seniors Spoil the Roth

Her older friends had warned her about it. I had referred to it once or twice, but nothing had quite prepared either of us for the shock of seeing it in black and white. On the day after my daughter's 50th birthday, she received the dreaded AARP letter. Now that she was officially a "senior," the word according to AARP, she was eligible to receive many of the same benefits her father and I did.

"Welcome to my world," I said out loud. But to myself, in a most unmotherly fashion, I was crying, "No, no, a thousand times no!" AARP notwithstanding, we can't all be seniors. Someone has to pay full price. With baby boomers crowding up the field, those of us who are legitimately old stand to lose everything we've fought for: discounts at movie theaters, schools, zoos, museums, airlines, railroads, retailers. These will be but fond memories as businesses do the math and find there are more of *us* than there are of *them*.

With apologies to my daughter and her friends, who, while bemoaning the age recognition, have not hesitated to put insurance companies on speed dial: something has to be done. The way things are going, Seniordom threatens to be the longest period of our lives. But there's such a wide gulf between a 50-year-old and a 70-year-old (I guarantee you, Cybill Shepherd's bottom line is a lot different from mine). It's time to recognize—there are seniors, and then there are *seniors.*

To deal with this problem, a few of us oldsters got together. We call ourselves CPA, the Committee to Preserve Aging, and we've come up with a plan that breaks down the category a little without losing the integrity of the brand.

We suggest calling the 50-to-60 group "junior seniors" with certain limited privileges attached: maybe $7 tickets to the movies instead of the regular $9 or $10 the youngsters under 50 pay? They might get 15 percent off skydiving and bungee-jumping equipment; *semi*-Elderhostels to Woodstock and Haight-Ashbury, plus membership in a new organization, AANRP (American Association of Nearly Retired Persons).

The 61-to-75 group could remain status quo: seniors as originally conceived. And ages 76 and up would have a whole new category: Senior Plus. Folks lucky enough to be this old would get the bulkhead seats on airplanes, double mileage for Florida flights, early-bird specials for cataract surgery, free tickets to movies, rocking chair concerts, and whatever perks their new organization, AAVRP (American Association of Very Retired Persons), can arrange.

Sound fair? We think so. And even if the government decides to let our children share our Medicare coverage, we oldsters can still look forward to our Senior Plus years. Whatever way you look at it, it's a when-when situation.

Out of Dates

Do you remember the good old days before expiration dates were stamped, embossed, or printed on practically every product we buy? I, for one, never worried about the future of my milk. When the butter, milk, cream smelled, I tossed it. Cheese moldy? Out. Crackers soft? Lose them. Eggs about to hatch? Abort. Meat a little brown around the edges? Don't chance it. But now, even if the cream still smells sweet, and the English muffins are as springy as a day in Blackpool, once that expiration date matches the calendar date, out they go. Who wants to tell a label where to get off?

If short-term expiration dates were the only problem, I could live with that. Even though I might wonder what happened to the week or two I was waiting for the milk to go sour, I wouldn't be wringing my hands and saying, "Where did the time go?" But when I am holding three dead AAA batteries I could swear I just replaced, all I can think of is: what was I doing for the two years those batteries were dying?

The thing is, not all time is created equal. We know this because when you make a dentist appointment a week in advance, before you can say "root canal," you're in the chair. But if you have to wait a week to find out if you got the job you want, a turtle could cross Times Square faster than those seven days. And if you really want to know about time, ask the woman who's in her ninth month of pregnancy, three days past her due date, how many hours are in each day.

That's why I'm so worried about my grocery closet. 2010 is beginning to look ominous. A quick survey shows my Cheerios will expire in December. My baking powder won't fizz after February. The yeast goes in March. I'm not sure what happens to granola, but it bites the dust in May. Only my cake flour can hold out until 2012, at which time yours truly will be two years older.

Consumer advocates who pushed for laws to protect us against spoilage probably thought they were doing us a favor. What they didn't foresee was that by predicting "the end" they were going to make time fly. I'm not saying they weren't good people, but we'd all be better off if they had seen the obvious. If something expires two or three years from now, and we know the exact date to the month, the time between now and then is going to go faster than time that doesn't have an end date on it. That's only common sense.

I just renewed my driver's license. It expires in 2014. And this brings me to the cause of my concern: if researchers can pinpoint the expiration date of a cornflake, or a Band-Aid, or a loaf of bread, who's next?

Make Room for Daddy

It all started when, quietly, almost apologetically, my husband decided to move in with me. For the 45 years of our marriage, we shared our home from seven in the evening to seven in the morning, plus all day Saturday, Sunday, and holidays. Then, all of a sudden, or what seemed like all of a sudden, there he was, with me, joined at the hip, from seven in the morning one day to seven in the morning the next. Just like that—sound of fingers snapping—he threw in the commuting towel and, in a brief statement, announced he was going to use the knowledge gained during his long career and become a consultant. "Good idea!" I enthused.

Five years ago, when he first complained about spending three hours on the train and fantasized about being semiretired and working from home, I was all for it. Why not? As empty nesters, we still had four bedrooms, three of them completely vacant except for a few leftover dolls. That's how I felt *then*. *Now*, it was a different story. I had long ago claimed the second bedroom in our two-bedroom condo as my office. In addition to my computer, printer, scanner, and file cabinets, I had my dictionaries, my thesaurus, my *Writer's Market*, my *PC for Dummies*, my *English for Dummies*, my *Networking for Dummies*, and all the other *Dummies* on bookshelves above and around my desk. I could certainly not be expected to share this crowded room. And my husband totally understood.

No problem, he said. I don't need much space, just a little corner to put a table (I won't even need a desk) for my computer, and maybe, if it's not too much trouble, a place to plug in my phone. We looked all around the premises (it didn't take long), and simple as his requirements seemed to be, we didn't know where to put him. The space that used to serve his home-time needs—the bedroom (he said it would make him sleepy working in there), the living room (he said it would ruin his ability to relax in the evening), and the kitchen table (we'd have to move the bananas)—didn't seem to make it as even a quasi-official office. There was only one place left: the dining room. Though not large, this oversize el did have a table and was next to a corner that could hold a file cabinet that could hold a printer. "Great," he said. "This is all I need."

How wonderful, I thought. What a strong marriage we have. And it might be fun. We'll both work in our respective "offices," and at lunchtime, he'll make his tuna fish sandwich (as soon as I show him how), and I'll make mine. Life will be the proverbial bowl of cherries without the pits. And so it was, at the beginning.

Having him and his little laptop at the dining room table wasn't too bad. I got used to seeing manila folders where the place mats used to be (I only put a wet glass down on one once). But as soon as his files were in place and his computer was set up, he began, ever so humbly, to "move into" my Internet access.

I say "my," because until that time, alone in the house, I was free to surf the Net at will, looking for any small piece of information I might need. We shared one account, with separate e-mail addresses, and my husband only "picked up" his mail at night when he came home from the office. Now I felt my spontaneity slipping away as business hours were spent with shouts of "are-you-ons" or "are-you-offs" until it no longer seemed worth going online.

We had to face the facts. Although we had shared many things in our lives (our bed, our bread), Internet access was not going to be one of them. After two weeks of yelling, we decided it would be better to have our accounts split than us. Pay the man the $23.90 a month.

Done. As always, we'd come to a sane, friendly arrangement. And things were going well for us, until I walked into the living room one day and noticed one of the end tables was missing. Now an end table is not something you mislay. And the lamp it had held, sitting on the floor, was a dead giveaway. Someone had taken it. That's when I noticed my husband's corner looked a little crowded. There, on the other side of the dining room table (his "office"), piled high with folders, pamphlets, and other accoutrements of a growing business, was the errant end table.

Apparently, he needed another file cabinet. As we canvassed the rooms yet again, I saw his eyes light on the corner close to the kitchen, where I had a small bookcase that held my cookbooks. "No, not there," I cried. "You wouldn't want your records to get splattered." Compromise time. "How about the garage?" I suggested gently. "They'll be safe there." His look of uncertainty was understandable considering his car was in the garage. Eventually, he came around when I reminded him the earth was warming, and even if our piece of it didn't, Triple-A was only a phone call away.

And that was that. I thought his thirst for expansion had been quenched, until one day I caught him in the entrance hall holding a measuring stick that looked as if it had been recently opened. He had that gleam in his eye, that I'm-bursting-out-of-my-corner look. I knew then he had other rooms in mind to conquer. Please, I prayed silently, anywhere, but not my office.

Whoever is in charge of household matters (or my prayers) must have had more urgent business, because not too long after the hall episode, I was working in my office when there was a light knock on the door. I knew who it was. My husband asked if he could come in and, clipboard in hand, said, "I have to look over some reports, would you mind if I used the chair in here? The light's better than in the dining room." Then this was it: the dining room, the living room, the garage, the hall. I knew it was over. In the distance, I could hear the whistle of the 8:15 train he used to waste three hours a day traveling on, as it whizzed by without him.

"Come in, come in," I insisted. "I've been expecting you."

Age Old

At the gym last week, I got into a discussion of age with a fellow swimmer and, for some reason, told her how old I am. Bad idea. She gasped, looked at me, and said with reverence, "God bless you."

Since I hadn't sneezed, I knew she was somehow praising me for making it to this advanced age, and suddenly I realized, I, who thought of myself as perhaps a little beyond middle age, was now at the "God bless you" stage of life. How could this be? Wasn't it just yesterday saleswomen, receptionists, complete strangers were bestowing their blessings on my mother-in-law (she was a spry 90 at the time) whenever the question of her age came up?

Something about longevity seems to inspire admiration approaching awe in those who have not yet reached a significant milestone themselves. If a couple announces on television they've been married for 50 years, the audience goes wild. Over 50, the cheers can be heard in the next studio. These days even 25 gets a good round of applause.

Why? For all anybody knows, the long-married couple may not have been all that happy. Maybe they wanted to divorce and only stayed together for the sake of the children. Or one spouse might have fallen off the fidelity track a few more times than he or she would care to remember. Or maybe it was always a marriage of convenience, and like 7-Eleven, they simply stayed open for business. Maybe theirs *was* an idyllic union, or maybe it *wasn't*, but remaining in a situation, in life or marriage, doesn't seem to me to be a cause for back patting by the observers or the observed. When I told my new friend my age, and she blessed me, she was, in her way, giving *me* the credit for still being around. But did I deserve it?

What assurance did she have I'd always crossed on the "green" and not in between, or taken my CoQ10 every day, or gotten flu shots every year? In addition to swimming, I might have been a tightrope walker and worked without a net or a bodysurfer on Maui or Oahu. Maybe I went on five-mile hikes on poor-air-quality days when old people were told not to risk it, or didn't keep my ears covered in the winter, or, throwing caution to the wind, allowed my face to brown under the lethal ultraviolet rays of the sun.

The point is, what had I actually done to deserve her blessing? (Aside from having lived through yet another death-defying birthday.) Imagine if I had told her my husband and I have been married for 56 years; the poor woman might have become totally undone.

I'm not one to refuse credit when I've accomplished something through my own efforts: like the time I got the blueberry stain out of a pink shirt (very, very hot water poured from a height with the fabric stretched over a glass), or finished the end-of-the-month *New York Times* crossword puzzle without looking up the capital of Bhutan (Thimphu), or won an argument with Medicare about paying for an unlisted drug.

I know my strengths, but I'm not sure old age can be counted as one of them. So, when I'm watching TV and see a bearded man, purported to be about 110, with white hair falling like a knotted fringe around his shoulders, sitting on a mountain in Tibet saying he owes his long life to the yogurt he's eaten each and every day, I have to wonder. One: is it the yogurt he's chosen to eat, or the mountain air that's made him live this agonizingly long? Two: how many of his childhood friends, who I assume must also have been candidates for this Dannon commercial, are still kicking around? And three: did he have anything to do with getting this high-paying gig? If he did, *then* I would proclaim, with heartfelt admiration, "God bless him."

Remembrance of Things Past

Some people give up meat; some people swear off Ben and Jerry's chocolate chip cookie dough ice cream; some people pour French wines down the drain. For myself, having just passed a significant birthday, I've decided to bite the bullet as firmly as I can these days and, as of this very moment, give up anything that looks like, tastes like, or smells like Self-Service.

I've had it. Fingers freezing on the hose, I've pumped my last gallon of gas, completed the final washing of my own windshield, vacuumed the last Goldfish crumbs from the floor of my sedan. Never again do I want to drive my car through a self-service car wash, water assaulting me from all sides while I struggle to keep myself and my car in neutral. From now on, it's the "service" side of the pump for me. "What's that you ask? Can you wash my windshield? Certainly, my good man, and please make sure to get the corners."

As for ATMs, or, as I like to think of them, the slot machines of the money world, forget it. Starting today, I'm going to walk into the bank like a real lady, give the teller my deposit or check, and let him or her do the number crunching. If we were meant to stand out in the rain or blinding sun to complete our bank business, why would there be all those fancy, dry, heated buildings with only the employees inside? And besides, I don't always *want* my cash in 20-dollar bills.

Sometimes, as I watch the last vestiges of service disappear faster than CEOs on Wall Street, and I'm feeling particularly paranoid, I wonder if some companies may secretly be hiring Service Reduction Managers whose job it is to figure our how to make life harder for us. Consider the salad bar. Did customers *demand* these self-service lettuce buffets? When you go out for a relaxing dinner at a restaurant, is it really worth the extra bacon bits to have to toss your own salad?

Did you ask to park your own car in the garage, driving round and round to find a spot on the *eighth* unheated level, while the "attendant" stays snug and cozy in his main-floor glassed-in office? *The New England Journal of Medicine* may not agree with me, but I'm convinced the reason we're all so tired is, after working a full day at our *own* jobs, we're asked to take on what should be someone *else's* job. The shoe salesperson *will*, at least at this writing, go into the stockroom and bring out the size and color you asked for, but you certainly can't expect her to stick around and remove all those wads of tissue that are inside the shoe or fit the shoe to your foot. That's not in her job description. Bending is strenuous, and she's saving *her* strength for shopping after work, in her own friendly neighborhood supermarket (the granddaddy of all self-service operations).

Unfortunately, I can't yet avoid supermarkets entirely (7-Elevens are not known for their meat), but I can draw a line in the sand, which leads me away from the latest machines designed to get us in and out of a store in a completely helpless manner. Last week, without so much as a what-would-you-think-of-this poll, my local market installed four self-service checkouts. Here you have the privilege to search for the bar code hidden on the last side you check of a six-sided package, weigh your bananas on the scanner/scale, and figure out how to insert your bills or credit card into the self-serving cashier. Now, it doesn't take a genius to know what's on these wily storekeepers' minds. First four machines, then eight, then not one human being to weigh your bananas or pack your bags. What's next? Anyone for restocking the shelves?

Count me out. I may not be able to turn the Tide (get it?), but I'm not going to let it wash over me either. As of now, I have a rotary phone (wink, wink), and I'll just have to "stay on the line for the next available representative." And if you're having trouble understanding me when I speak, it's because I've swallowed the card that has my PIN number on it, and 3265 is forever gone from my memory. But again, no problem. I won't be needing it anymore. Read my lips: the operative word here is "help," and even my family agrees, I need plenty of it.

Time Out

Stop! Enough! Can't we take a few decades' breather? Doesn't anybody have anything better to do than think of more advances in technology? I consider myself a pretty hip chick. My computer skills are awesome (now). I can find out what's playing at the movies and even buy tickets online. I can *almost* use my scanner, and I'm on the verge of burning my own CDs. As for me and my digital camera, at least once a week I send adorable pictures of my grandchildren to all of my friends who have computers and make prints for those who don't.

But every time I think I've caught up, prepared for the next step, technology takes a giant leap, and I'm three generations behind again. My cell phone is just that—a phone with enough cells of some kind to let me make or receive calls when I'm in my car or walking along the street and want to let my friend know I'm turning left. It doesn't take pictures of me or anyone else, nor does it keep track of my appointments, or show texts, or play music, or double as a walkie-talkie. It's only a few years old, and when I pull it out of my bag, I might as well have a rotary phone.

As for my camcorder, it's been around the world with me, and I thought I was taking pretty good videos, but what did I know? It turns out my megapixel count is an embarrassment. With as few pixels as I've got, it's amazing my dots connect at all.

If I could trust pixel counts to stay put for a while, I'd trade up. But I know from past experience, today's "megas" are tomorrow's "minis," and I'd have no resolution to my problem.

Keeping up with advances in television sets is made more complicated by the extensive use of initials. This should come as no surprise because these instruments of entertainment have been referred to as TVs from the very beginning. So now it turns out, we should have LCDs for our TVs or, better yet, TFT-LCDs, and our sets should be HDTV ready. And how important is CGMS to me? Would any of these show up on a screen that is only semi-flat?

What worries me is, I don't know enough about what I should be worrying about. Not only can't I imagine what's coming, I don't have a clue about what's already "in" and about to be declared "out." Here's my idea: despite all the money drug companies have poured into finding a cure for the common cold, and automobile companies have invested in developing fuel-efficient cars, and power companies have sunk into creating new sources of energy, we're still sniffling, using mega gallons of gas, and burning oil as if we owned the Middle East. Couldn't we redirect some of those techies who, as we speak, are working on a fax machine that sings "Dixie," and engage them in solving some of these more urgent problems? Maybe they wouldn't come up with the answers right away, but at least we'd have some time to figure out what all the initials mean before they, and we, become hopelessly obsolete.

Age Less

My mother viewed the term *senior citizen* as a pejorative. I think she was somewhere around 65 herself when the phrase came into use. And she was not about to admit to the government or anybody else that she fit into that category. She lost a number of eligible years before applying to Medicare or carrying anything in her wallet that had the word *senior* on it.

Her age, or that of her sisters or her mother, was not something she or we ever talked about. Through innuendo, sly smiles, and vague allusions, we children were given to understand Aunt Marguerite, the oldest sister, was *much older* than one would ever guess, and my mother, the youngest, must have been a mere *child* when she and my father were married if she had children as grown-up as we were.

In the thirties, my mother was not an anomaly. Most movie actresses were at least 10 years older than they said they were. Models who looked 18 were 30. And a little fib to one's husband about one's birth date was not uncommon. At that time, "Never ask a woman's age" was an accepted part of the social contract.

Still, many of my friends knew their mothers' ages and talked freely about them, which made me think there was something mystical about age in our family. Were we somehow excused from the aging process? At 9 or 10, I looked about the same as any other 9- or 10-year-old, but when, I wondered, would it stop? When would I *not* get the telltale wrinkles I should have? Or worse, would I be the only one in the family who didn't look much younger than "we were"? To me, the mystery was tantalizing, and try as I would, in the case of my mother, I never found out what the "we were" was.

When my brother married at 24 (I did know his age) and became a father a year later, my mother, in the natural course of things, became a grandmother at the tender age of ____. We all knew she was too young to be a grandmother; how *much* "too young" we weren't sure. We accepted her pronouncement without question though, and her first grandchild and those following called her "Nana," a kind of nebulous term—warm, but not age-specific, nothing rocking-chair or gray-haired about it.

Speaking of gray hair, this was another unmentionable. Not too many grandmothers allowed "silver threads among the golden" to show. "Only her hairdresser knows for sure" was a much-quoted slogan of the time. If a woman did have gray hair, it usually had a slight blue cast to it, which, I suppose, was meant to convey the impression her hair was dyed silver by choice, indicating she wasn't old enough for her hair to have naturally turned that color. My mother's hair was always kept to a "natural" brunette, which grew inexplicably lighter as the years went on.

When any changes occurred in her life, we always got the impression it happened or was happening to her much earlier than to anyone else. She got married earlier, had children earlier, went through "The Change" earlier. Somehow, she even had us convinced she began collecting Social Security before she was 62. No birth certificates were left lying around our house, so proving one's suspicions was not a possibility.

Vanity, per se, was only part of the reason my mother was reluctant to talk about age. She had a great dread of being considered old-fashioned. Maybe it was the word *old* that bothered her. In her mind, to be slotted as a *senior citizen* or a *grandmother* was to be isolated from the mainstream. Although she was never in the workplace, she was ahead of her time in thinking about age bias. It was her feeling that all her creative thoughts and ideas would lose value if the age of their source were generally known.

In order to protect this ongoing secret, my mother never harked back to the good old days. She viewed looking back as the surest sign of age. There were no when-I-was-a-girls or I-remember-whens in her conversation. I would have liked hearing about gaslights, or iceboxes, or horse-driven trolley cars, or what New York looked like in 1915. This wasn't possible, though, because to talk about life in the early years of the century meant admitting she had been there, and that was not going to happen.

While my mother was reluctant to *talk* about her age, she always seemed to dress and act appropriately for a woman in her _____ies. That is, when I was a teenager, she wasn't wearing bobby socks or saddle shoes. In fact, she was quite contemptuous of women who tried to be "kittenish." She herself could be described as mature, but not to her face. *Mature* was another word she did not particularly like.

Naturally, there came a time when she had to acknowledge a certain degree of seniority. If she was unable to do as much cooking or baking as she used to, she would never come right out and say, "It's because I'm getting old." She might look at you, after admitting to some fatigue, and say, "I'm getting older, you know," and then wait for the look of disbelief in your eyes, a sign you hadn't really noticed. But, of course, we had noticed. We just never let on.

I, on the other hand, have always enjoyed announcing to all who would listen how old I am. If there is an age-denial gene, I didn't get it. Or it might be a lingering teenage rebellion thing, or a don't-mistake-me-for-my-mother statement. I'm not sure. What I do know is, I've always celebrated my birthdays, particularly the milestones—30, 40, 50, and up—out loud. That's not to say I am without my vanity. When I was 70, and the bus driver asked to see proof I was a senior before he would allow me to pay the reduced fare, my whole family heard about it and once again marveled at how young *we* looked, even when *we* were old—er.

After my mother died, I found her birth certificate among her papers. I was shocked to find she didn't marry *that* young, or have children *that* young, or become a grandmother at an unusually young age. Of course, in my heart, she died too young. But she was, after all, _____ years of age.

Open-and-Shut Case

Every time the average life expectancy age goes up (it has now reached 81 for women, 76 for men), I think of how many more people won't be able to open a jar of pickles.

While medical researchers have been running their lab rats ragged trying to prolong their lives, and ultimately ours, the rest of society has been moving even faster to create a world in which these lucky septuagenarians and octogenarians can't function.

If you don't believe me, take a hard look at bubble packs. It's obvious. Whoever thought of this bum wrapping hated his parents. Why else would you create a package that requires an ax to hack it open? (Was Lizzie Borden really a monster or just trying to open a box of paper clips?) When the tough plastic bubbles first appeared as the package of choice, I thought I could avoid buying anything that was encased in this unbreakable material. But I soon found that would mean I couldn't buy a camera, a battery, a pen, an action figure, an electric razor, a hair dryer, a USB cable, a calculator, a clock-radio, a hairbrush, a meat thermometer, a picture frame, a book light, an ink cartridge, travel Scrabble, a food scale, an electric toothbrush, a curling iron, goggles, a Dustbuster.

The picture I had of retirement didn't include hours spent trying to release newly purchased items from their plastic cages. It's one thing to get the thermometer out of the package and into the turkey breast on Thanksgiving morning; it's quite another to desperately need a Pepcid and a half hour later still be trying to pop the little pill from its well-sealed bubble.

At first glance, the package seems harmless, better than the foam popcorn that covers the floor like the first indoor snowfall of the season. And no one can deny the protection it affords a fragile product. Who knows what would happen to a cordless phone if it were left unbubbled in an old-fashioned cardboard box? On the other hand, has any one considered the damage that can be done to a product on the inside when the frustrated new owner is trying every conceivable device to pry it open? Knife? Screwdriver? Awl? A perforated ink cartridge is not a pretty sight.

If the Maker designated a corner to pull, pinch, or peel, using a large indelibly stamped arrow to confirm the whereabouts of the opening, those of us whose tensile strength has been compromised over the years might have a fighting chance of getting to the product. Unfortunately, the area most vulnerable to tinkering is left to the opener's imagination, so the odds are high against your getting to the hair dryer before your hair dries or to the alarm clock before it's time to get up.

Without flexing my senior muscles too boldly, I would like to remind manufacturers, the baby boomers and I are going to be buying a large portion of your products. So I think it's well within my purview to ask: what are you going to do for openers?

An Old Wife's Tale

I have no problem with people making their own mistakes, but why should my children or grandchildren make mine? It hurts me to stand by and watch members of the younger generation throw caution to the wind, walk under ladders (or cranes), allow black cats to cross their paths, toss hats on the bed without giving so much as a nod to what may happen later in the day.

What I say to my progeny is: we don't have much control over events in our lives (it may rain on our parade at any time), so why tempt fate? If it's your wedding day, and your mother has warned you: sing before seven, cry before eleven, would it hurt to hold it down until after the ceremony?

Doesn't it make sense to cover all bases? You are hardworking, dedicated, and about to reach your goal, why let the milk boil over? You may not totally believe your "reckless" behavior will bring you bad luck; still, can you be absolutely sure it won't? Are you willing to take that chance?

My family should certainly be aware of what can happen when one of nature's promises is messed with. I've told them the story often enough: why I stayed 5'2" when all around me continued to grow into lanky teenagers and giant adults. I was 9 or 10 years old (and by the way, the tallest girl in fifth grade), lying on my back in the gym, ready to begin an exercise, when someone stepped over my outstretched legs. Just like that, no warning, *boom*, and my fate was sealed. Alice Moskowitz said so. Her grandmother had told her mother, and she told me, if someone steps over your outstretched legs, your growth will be stunted. This was not a superstition, she insisted, this was a known fact. I wasn't sure of Alice's warnings then, but now, 60-odd years later, when I have to stand on my tiptoes to kiss even my youngest grandchild good night, I have to admit she knew what she was talking about.

That's why, once I found out by stepping on a crack I could break my father's back, I carefully avoided even the smallest crack in the sidewalk when I was growing up in the city. Was it a coincidence my father never even had lower back pain? Perhaps. Or was I the best daughter ever?

In all fairness, if anyone asked me (an unlikely scenario), did I personally know someone who suffered bad luck after placing his shoes on a table, I would have to say, "No, I've only heard about it." You have to wonder, though, how would such a rumor get started if someone's day had not been ruined following such a shoe-placing episode?

Despite my feelings about unearthly sources at work, I'd be the last one to advise my children to just sit back and accept as fate the consequences of their actions. What I'm saying is, show a little respect for any sign nature throws your way. Walk carefully. Don't kill any more ladybugs than you have to. Avoid spilling salt (and if you do, throw some over your left shoulder). Never open your umbrella in the house (unless the roof is leaking).

Some forces are harder to deal with and harder to understand. I'm as baffled by the mysteries of the universe as the next guy. Am I sure dropping and shattering my hand mirror had anything to do with my breaking out in hives just before we went on vacation? Who knows? *But* I haven't used a hand mirror since, and my skin has been smooth as a baby's.

Good luck omens are a lot easier sell than bad. Whose day is not a little brighter for having picked a four-leaf clover from a field of three-leafers? Or who doesn't get the connection between his palm itching in the morning and a sizable check arriving FedEx in the afternoon? I don't know a single person who doesn't cross her fingers or knock on wood when making a happy announcement. And anyone who sneezes three times before breakfast or accidentally puts her dress on inside out is usually perfectly willing to believe the day ahead will be glorious.

That said, to my deep consternation, I sometimes detect a whiff of skepticism even among my own family members. This came to light when a young whippersnapper (one of my own) accused me of still believing the tooth fairy would leave a quarter under my pillow when I had my impacted wisdom tooth extracted last year. Patently false. Anyone who knows me will tell you I have my two feet planted firmly on the ground, and that's why I've had a lot of good fortune in my life. While looking down at my feet to make sure they're still firmly planted, every so often

I spot a penny. Nonbelievers would say, in this day and age, it isn't worth the bend to pick it up. Not me.

See a penny, pick it up,
All day long, you'll have good luck.

And not counting the time I threw my back out (it was a bad angle), by and large, it's worked, *and* I have a considerable number of pennies, in case I ever have to buy bubble gum for a crowd.

I know there will always be some people out there who do not share my cause-and-effect beliefs. If you're one of them and you're wondering why *my* parsley plant is so much bigger than *yours*, I can only say:

Where the mistress is the master,
The parsley grows the faster.

ON HEALTH

Though health is a topic
We seniors relate to,
Advice given freely
Can make people hate you.

Supplemental Information

Ten years ago if you had asked me what an antioxidant was, I probably would have said it was something you put on silver to keep it from tarnishing. When I heard the term *free radicals*, I was ready to fight for their immediate release. What can I tell you? I was so nutritionally illiterate I actually thought my One a Day Plus Iron would fill in the gaps on the days my only vegetable was the iceberg lettuce that lined a ham on white. Mea culpa.

It wasn't until all the wellness newsletters began arriving in the mail, and vitamin infomercials cropped up on television, and a myriad of books on nutrition flooded the bookstore, that I found out what my body had probably been crying for all these years. Supplements. Supplements. Supplements.

Once I realized that by taking a mere 15 to 20 little pills a day, I could prevent or retard bone loss, dry skin, muscle aches, baldness, fatigue, anxiety, constipation, insomnia, and at the same time enhance my liver function, sex drive, appetite, complexion, metabolism, my blood began to rush unhampered through my veins.

As I swallow my supplements each morning, I can

practically feel the hair growing on my head. It only takes me about 15 minutes to wash down 1,500 mg of garlic, 400 IU of vitamin E, 10,000 IU of vitamin A, 400 IU vitamin D, 40 mg zinc, 600 mg vitamin C, 200 mg selenium, 500 mg echinacea, 1,500 mg calcium, 750 mg glucosamine, 150 mg CoQ10, and 1,000 mg bee pollen. CoQ10 is a particularly costly whatever-it-is, but as one nutritionist put it recently, "Can you put a price on being able to tie your own shoelaces when you're a hundred years old?"

There are supplemental skeptics who insist we can get all the extra nutrients we need from so-called enriched products: cereal, pasta, bread. No offense meant, but I question their reasoning. How can we be sure the ABCs, to name a few, are *in* there? And if they *are*, how did they *get* there? Is each flake of Total injected with the 19 nutrients listed on the box? Are they sprayed on? Or are they put in a paper bag with the flakes and shaken up, while a proud worker stands by and shouts, "All the vitamins are in and *Ah* helped."

Knowing what I now know, I would hate to trust my well-being to some ghost nutrients nobody in my crowd has ever seen. And I think the condition of my body speaks for itself. Even a casual observer, noting my luxuriant hair, my flawless complexion, my trim waist would know I'm on something. How else could you explain the spring in my step, my arms moving rhythmically, up, down, up, down, if not for all the joint looseners and motor enhancers I swallow whole?

Maybe, just maybe, I could get by on green leafy vegetables, nonfat milk solids, and 16-grain bread. And maybe

I could kick the molybdenum and—heaven help me—the omega-3 fatty acids and just concentrate on salmon and buckwheat pancakes. Maybe I could, and maybe my eyelashes would curl on their own, but it wouldn't be me. I know myself, and the truth of the matter is, I've just never been one to go in for fads.

Your Ad Dollars at Work

Hospital bills today can be out of sight. A thousand dollars a day for a semiprivate room, not including the box of tissues on the bedside table, is at the low end of the scale. So how come we are bombarded with ads for hospitals advertising for patients? "We have a *great* Intramuscular Center," the announcer proclaims. "Come on down to Westchester (New Jersey, Long Island)."

Now I believe in advertising. I do. Whenever I hear what sounds like a great product described on the radio, I'm tempted to pull my car over, leap out, and rush into the nearest store. That goes for spot removers, spaghetti sauce, and fat-free doughnuts. But when the product is a hospital, and I, a tried-and-true Nutmegger, am being asked to consider Massachusetts Central for my next brain tumor operation, heaven forbid! I do have to pull over to the side of the road, but not to shop.

To begin with, my home in Connecticut may be 200 miles from Mass Central or Hoboken Memorial or Eastern Long Island Surgery. And though it sounds mighty tempting, I'm not sure if I (spit three times) or any of my loved ones should become metastasized, we would want to drive hundreds of miles to a hospital to be an outpatient for radiation therapy or some of the other really great-sounding noninvasive surgical procedures.

Get real. The mellifluous tones and jaunty copy can't disguise the depressing product. How appealing can you make a heart transplant sound? Am I going to go racing toward Eastern Poultice because I heard a satisfied customer extolling the virtues of a hospital that gave him the bloodless operation he sought for his enlarged prostate? Is anyone going to risk raising an already high blood pressure driving in traffic to reach a distant medical facility that wants the chance to treat her hypertension?

These ad guys sure know how to ruin a day. Here you are, riding along in your car, enjoying a bright sunny afternoon in the country, great music coming from your favorite station and—*shazam*! This commercial comes on: "Do you have trouble eating, sleeping, or getting out of bed in the morning? Do things look bleak and hopeless? If you have any or all of these symptoms, you may be suffering from clinical depression, and if so, you may qualify to participate in a research study now taking place at South Jersey Laboratories." Goody. What's second prize?

Sometimes, it's a Jeopardy scenario. Category: Health. Answer: Diabetes. Question: Do you know what the leading cause of blindness is in the country? I do now.

I wonder how many people are moved to action by a voice trying to sell hormone therapy for osteoporosis or angioplasty for that pesky blocked artery, or asking you if you've had a really good MRI recently?

It was my impression hospitals were hard-pressed

to find money for Jell-O these days, let alone the wherewithal to wage an aggressive ad campaign. If a hospital has to fill its rooms by wooing away customers from its own neighborhood health centers, if it has to advertise for patients and make open-heart surgery sound like getting the stains out of a cashmere sweater, could it be we have too many hospitals? Or is it just a playing out of the American Dream?

In this country, even a walk-in treatment center can aspire to long-term care. So if a hospital wants to buy radio time to tell the world about its gangbuster embolism team, and it has to scrimp a little on the cotton balls and Lysol, who am I to interfere with freedom of advertising? But I have my freedoms, too, and one of them is the freedom to switch stations. Another is to make sure my next car's radio comes with a prominently displayed, easily reached mute button.

Ask Your Doctor About

At last count I receive four wellness letters a month—two from local hospitals, one from a distinguished university, and a women's health newsletter from an alternative medicine group in Vermont where I once stopped to buy maple syrup. Add that to my familiarity with the latest advances in the treatment of cancer, heart disease, acid reflux, stroke (I turn to the science section of the paper first), 15 seasons of *ER*, six of *Grey's Anatomy*, and only Nielsen knows how many of *Marcus Welby, M.D.* (may he rest in peace). Add to that a lifetime subscription to *Prevention Magazine*, and you have someone who, most people would agree, is full of it.

Having all this valuable information at my sometimes numb fingertips has allowed me to make my own carefully considered medical decisions. Home-schooled as I may be, with the degree on my bathroom wall reading, "Bachelor of Arts," I still have little reason to consult my doctor. Even if he were willing to come to the phone the same day I called, it would be a total waste of his valuable time. Who knows better than I what my symptoms are and what immediate steps are to be taken? Why only last month there was an article in *Consumer Diagnostics* telling me how to distinguish heart-related chest pain from sneeze-related chest pain. If I decide it's a matter of the heart, I will have to bother my M.D. for a prescription for Procardia, assuming it has an angina origin. If I decide it's just a muscle spasm, I'll take two aspirin (which incidentally is not too shoddy a treatment for the early stages of stroke or a myocardial infarction), and if the pain lasts three or more days, I'll consult my physician—or the latest copy of *Arthritis Today*, whichever comes first.

Luckily, for those of us who have taken seriously the oft-repeated words, "Today, you have to be your own doctor," medical information is available not only on TV but in every possible printed form (Amazon lists 116,272 books on the subject). So if you can't sleep at night (there are multiple reasons for this: stress, too much caffeine, bad mattress), just visit HealthFinder.gov, MayoClinic.com, or any one of the other 2,550,000,000 health-information sites Google will come up with in .09 seconds. No lay doctor could wish for more information than is provided, free of charge, without prescription, on the Web. Whatever your ailment, be it anything from adenoids to warts, as long as you know what letter it begins with, you can find it, along with links to scientific articles pertaining to recommended treatments, approved medications, and centers that specialize in your disease.

So far this year, I've made in-depth studies of hypertension, bird flu, Lyme disease, and ingrown toenails. I've checked out all the drugs I'm taking to guard against harmful interactions (actually, I only take one, a statin, so grapefruits are out for me). In the process, I've learned a lot of new names that will come in handy when I'm trying to find out what drug will make me more "normal."

That's why I am ever so grateful to all the pharmaceutical companies, bloggers, and undocumented health experts for letting me know, almost daily, what's new on the market in both conditions and treatments. They seem sure that despite my lack of formal medical education—a mere technicality—I will know how to evaluate the latest research findings. And if, by any chance, I find myself a little uncertain about what to do with all the information being thrown at me, I can always ask my doctor, who, I'm sure, will have no trouble telling me what to do with it.

Strong Medicine

It's no wonder doctors are up in arms about drug companies advertising directly to the consumer. So many of the drug commercials on radio and television are so unbelievably tempting, I, for one, hardly know what to choose. Should it be Potocan, a new entry on the drug market that would do wonders for my neuralgia and have only minimal side effects (loss of balance, memory, and hearing)? Or would I be better off with Vandacor, which is less likely to put me in a coma?

This new marketing strategy of advertising prescription drugs to the consumer is really smart. The drug companies have finally learned from their fellow peddlers how to sell a product. Create a demand. Promote the product in such a way that I, the consumer, am dying (figuratively speaking) to get it. Those hucksters know if I hear that a 92-year-old woman who was bedridden for 10 years took Exoflexochlorizine and started to disco, I'm going to beg my doctor to GIVE ME THAT DRUG.

I want *it* for the same reason I want a new silver polish I saw advertised on TV—they say it will make my silver cleaner and brighter than whatever I'm using now.

Mind you, I have no complaints about my old silver polish. But if I can get it still shinier, I'm going to buy it. Even if the label says it may corrode the silver when left on for more than one and a quarter minutes, even if I have to wear gloves to protect my hands from acid burn and use a shield for my eyes in the unlikely event they're sensitive to Anipolydrozamine.

The only difference between buying the new silver polish and a drug is that I don't need a prescription to get the polish. This prescription thing is a bother. I shouldn't need someone else's undecipherable handwriting on letterhead to buy what I need for my condition. I'm perfectly able to diagnose my own symptoms and choose suitable medication. I subscribe to some of the most distinguished health newsletters, I read Jane Brody religiously, and I can find all the supplementary information I need on the Internet. The powers that be who want to keep this drug prerogative to themselves should wake up. Doctors must understand, in this day of overworked physicians struggling to see enough patients to satisfy the health-plan people, we consumers have to take charge of our own cases. I'm sure my doctor tries to keep up with all the latest advances in medicine, but when it comes right down to it, how much time does he really have to watch TV or listen to the radio?

Though some might say the drug companies would be better off putting their dollars into research and forgetting advertising, I disagree. There are some major players out there and I want to know about them. How else can I tell my doctor what he should prescribe? And although he's never found words to express it, I'm sure he really appreciates my letting him know there's a better drug on the market than the one he's been handing out. Picking products on the basis of advertising is my thing! I've been highly successful in treating my dry scalp, the spots on my carpet, my lackluster toilet bowls, so why not my gallbladder?

I've always been a feminist—to a certain extent. I believe in equal pay for equal work and all the big stuff, but starting with Year One of our marriage, more than 50 years ago, my husband and I both knew who would be taking out the garbage or walking the dog early in the morning and late at night. Nor was there ever any question about who would drop whom off at the door of the theater or restaurant if it was raining.

My husband suffered a stroke five years ago, and when the blow came, if someone were to ask who was now going to stand on a ladder and change the bulb in the garage or use a plunger on uncooperative plumbing, my name would not spring readily to mind. Many friends, who came to the hospital when the dark days following the stroke had begun to lighten and my husband was relearning the once automatic skills of standing, walking, and talking, said, with the wisdom of having lived through similar experiences, your life will never be the same.

At the time, I considered the ominous words in cosmic terms. Obviously, we were not going to go on hiking trips through the Himalayas, but then we had never gone on hiking trips through the Himalayas. What nobody mentioned (and I wasn't prepared for) was the kind of lesser event that happened the night before my husband was due to come home from the rehab center. It was ten o'clock at night and raining outside. When I opened the door to the condo, the indoor temperature was 43 degrees and, to my great dismay, our heat was off.

The serviceman who answered my frantic call to the oil company asked, "Did you try the reset button?" Although I had personally never pushed one, I had seen my husband do it and knew it was located on the furnace, which was in our second garage. There was no access from the condo. To push it would require going out in the rain, in the dark, creeping in and finding first the furnace, then the little red button. Instinctively, I looked around to see if there was anyone else to send. Finding no one, I made the unlikely journey, pressed the button, and to my great amazement—*wham*—the furnace turned on. Wet but exhilarated, I returned to the phone and reported: mission accomplished. I, a card-carrying JAP,[1] had restored heat to our home.

That was only the beginning. Though my husband grew stronger every day, there were still many things he could not do. Drive, for one. I became the sole director of transportation. Now, rain or shine, it was I who dropped my husband off at the door and parked the car in some remote part of a dimly lit lot. And when the gas gauge indicated fill 'er up or be stranded on the way home, no

1 Jewish American Princess: one who is cajoled, coddled, and catered to by her parents, and then cajoled, coddled, and catered to by her husband.

one was more surprised than I that I could brave the elements, pump the gas, and even extract the receipt for my credit card payment. We're talking reborn here.

My taking over, so to speak, was not easy for my husband either. Although technically he could not steer the car, he still remained in the driver's seat, if you know what I mean. He remembered the shortest route from here to there and reminded me as I took each "wrong" turn. He also remembered the speed limit for all the local roads, something I apparently had forgotten.

As time went on, he continued to hone my driving skills, keep me up to date on the garbage schedule, and offer advice on how much of a tip to leave in the restaurant when I was paying the check. Most of the time—well, some of the time—I didn't mind the quarterbacking, because it was an indication of his steady improvement from the effects of the stroke.

And I was making some strides, too. My muscles strengthened to the point where I could lift a 40-pound bag off the carousel at the airport; another one of my newly acquired skills was finding the circuit breaker that controlled the electricity for the upstairs bedroom when the lights went out.

We were both coming along nicely, and on the day of our wedding anniversary, our first since the stroke, an especially bright light broke through the clouds. A beautiful basket of flowers arrived at the door. They were from my husband. Willing the fingers on his right hand to punch in the numbers, he had dialed 1-800-FLOWERS and ordered the bouquet all by himself. First I cried looking at them, knowing how hard it must have been for him to accomplish this once simple task and how much he must have wanted to do it. But then I smiled, because I realized, though the division of labor had shifted a bit and I was now doing the heavy lifting, our actual roles had not changed since Day One. Here was the blooming proof. In his own hard-fought way, *he*, my husband, was still looking after *me*.

Fit for Life

The Institute of Medicine now says Americans should exercise one hour a day (that's twice the amount previously recommended, and three times the amount recommended before that, when the experts felt 20 minutes a day, five times a week—or was it five minutes, four times a day, or 10 minutes twice a day—would be beneficial), but only if you're careful about what exercise you do and when you do it, and everyone agrees—

swimming is the best exercise, unless you want to prevent osteoporosis, in which case you'll have to build upper-body strength by lifting weights, remembering that weight lifting is not aerobic and aerobic exercise is vital for circulation, which is why you have to jog, walk, or cycle, preferably before eating, because you have to wait at least an hour after eating to engage in any vigorous pursuit—

especially since the time you eat and what you eat is crucial to your well-being, and you must get those carbs in for extra energy, unless you're one of those people who doesn't do well with carbs and needs more protein and fiber, and of course we all need more fiber, and remember that the sugar you find in those eight helpings of fruit and vegetables is not the same as the sugar in a jelly doughnut, one of which has more fat than an average person needs in a week, except for those fish fats you can't get enough of since they're better than meat—

which, though technically a protein, is completely unnecessary in a healthy diet replete with beans and grains, including rice—never white, always brown—and soy products, sometimes shown to decrease calcium and vitamin D, which of course you can replace with dairy products like yogurt, cheese, sour cream—

unless you have a cholesterol problem, in which case you want to keep away from whole milk or whole eggs and switch to some of the substitutes on the grocery shelves that replace fat with a few chemicals you may want to avoid if you're worried about your liver or blood pressure that is sure to go up with an excessive intake of the sodium found in prepared soups, frozen dinners, soy sauce, Worcestershire sauce, tomato sauce, crackers, salted nuts, and salami—also high in saturated fats, which are worse than monounsaturated fats but equal to polyunsaturated fats, to be avoided at all costs, though not at the price of causing tension or worry, two harmful emotions that wreak such havoc on your body (lower your immune system, cause impaired vision and insomnia, intensify allergic reactions) that even if you exercise, exchange all meats and dairy products for organically grown vegetables and avoid McDonald's like the plague, they will kill you in the end.

10,000 Steps
or
A Walk in the Parking Lot

My last visit to the ophthalmologist's office changed my life. Not because I found out I could no longer read *a t v e n z q s* on the third row from the bottom, but because while waiting for the drops to take effect, I was attracted to a magazine with an intriguing headline on its cover: "10,000 Steps to a Longer, Healthier Life."

Drawn in by the promise I might one day be in Willard Scott's One-Hundred-Year-Old Club, I turned to page 22, where the story began. There each sentence bulged with evidence supporting the claim. My heart, my lungs, my blood vessels were crying out for me to take the necessary steps. No special equipment or expensive lessons were needed. All I had to do was put on my sneakers and walk.

But (and I had a big but) could I do it? I am now, and for many years have been, a devout suburbanite. I don't walk, I drive . . . everywhere—to the mailbox, to the supermarket a block away, to my exercise class, a half block from the supermarket. When I park, I circle until I get a spot as close to where I'm going as possible. I even give myself points for closeness: 10 points, right in front of the door; 9 points, one space removed, and so on. Anything below a 6, I circle.

So despite my enthusiasm, I realized it would be a challenge for me to rack up enough steps to break 1,000, much less 10 big ones. But because I've always harbored a secret desire to live to 100, and the article said stepping out more might improve my chances, I decided to spring for a pedometer ($3.83 plus tax) and get started on my life-enhancing program.

The directions that came with it were simple. I was told first to walk 10 steps, then measure the distance I had walked, divide that by 10 and—voilà—I would have my stride. Next, I was to clip this little instrument to the waistband of my skirt or pants, and I would be ready to go.

Happily, the instruction manual took a reasonable approach. "Don't expect to reach your goal overnight," it cautioned. "Increase your activity gradually, maybe 400 steps a day over 12 days until you reach your goal: 10,000 steps." I was psyched.

My first day's score was a downer: 3,262 steps, even though I attached my pedometer to my pajamas as soon as I got out of bed. Could there have been a misprint in the manual? Was it possible my waist didn't move as often as my legs, which resulted in a step shortage? Since nothing in the manual seemed to deal with unusual body types, I decided to get on with my measurements.

Immediately, I knew we should have bought a bigger house. I couldn't believe it was only 40 steps from my bedroom to my office upstairs. And I didn't get anything extra if I stopped and put two feet on each step. Walking around the living and dining rooms, in what now seemed a Lilliputian-size home, added only another 74 steps, leaving 9,886 to reach my final goal. By circling the living room/dining room twice before going to work, I was able to reduce that to 9,812. Better, but what other steps could I take?

The burbs hold two opportunities for walking: the super-supermarket and the mall. Before my epiphany, I had been known to complain about the size of the market. If I forgot the mayo and was already at paper napkins, I had to walk clear across what seemed like miles back to Aisle 1, then back again to Aisle 13. I'm embarrassed to say, I didn't realize, by making the store as inconvenient as possible, the store designers were only thinking of my health. Instead of moaning about the huge space, as I had done previously, I welcomed the fatigue that comes from going back and forth, and in and out, of the aisles, trying to find a box of Kleenex. To me, now, it was more than just an exhausting place, it was an arena where I could add as many as 2,500 steps, plus 500 or 600, on a bad-memory day.

The mall, too, is a walker's paradise. I can only dream of how many steps lie between Macy's and JCPenney, the department stores that anchor the ends. Someday, I may tackle that marathon; for now, I relished the 785 steps it takes to go from the entrance of the mall, through an entire floor of Lord & Taylor, to the center plaza. By the time I walked from Victoria's Secret to Banana Republic, then to the Gap and Ann Taylor, my pedometer was practically jumping for joy: 3,978 steps. Count them! And I hadn't even bought anything!

The adjoining parking lots of both the supermarket and the mall hold as many steps as I thought they did. To reach the magical 10,000, I had to completely reverse my point system. Now the further away I parked, the more points I gave myself. Actually, it was no trouble at all finding a spot yards and yards away from the entrance, particularly on a rainy day. The good news was I added to my daily total more than 300 steps each way. Because of my modest beginnings, it took me almost four weeks to see those big numbers on my little pedometer. Knowing how interested my family, friends, and possibly others would be in the strides I made, I kept a daily diary. The following is a detailed account of the day I went over the top:

Bedroom to office: 40
Living room/dining room (twice): 148
Desk to bookshelf: 24
Office to refrigerator (twice): 92
Mailbox and back: 446
Supermarket to exercise class: 758
Exercise class back to car: 475
Inside supermarket: 2,855
Supermarket parking lot (round-trip): 558
In the mall: 3,978
Mall parking lot (round-trip): 632

10,006

No doubt about it, I credit my eye doctor with changing my life. Since I started counting my steps, I eat more, because I'm craving those extra 46 steps to the fridge. I buy more, because I'm spending more time in the supermarket. And the mall is a constant temptation. (My heart rate might be up not so much from the walking but because I see so many things I can't afford to buy.) As for my longevity, it's too early to tell. Although at the end of a 10,000-plus day, 100 doesn't seem so very far away.

Diets I Have Known

The reason I don't want to lose 10 pounds in 10 days, or take 2 inches off my waist in 2 weeks, or shed 15 pounds before the summer is: I've been there, done that. You name it, I've tried it.

Long before Weight Watchers was even a gleam in Jean Nidetch's eye, I had been on the Metropolitan Diet, three well-planned, small-portioned meals using all seven food groups with discretion; the Ry Krisp Diet, three well-planned, small-portioned meals using all seven food groups with discretion, and myriad others with and without official names.

In my teens, I heard of one that would help you lose a lot of weight if you limited yourself to eating one food all day. I chose chocolate milk shakes. I had one for breakfast, one for lunch, and one for dinner—and sometimes one before going to bed. And boy did I lose weight, not so much from the one-food idea as from throwing up everything I had eaten for the two weeks before. It was a full week before I gained the weight back.

Then there was the Drinking Man's Diet. I didn't drink

and I wasn't a man, but I did love steak and that's what this diet was all about. Meat! All the steak you could eat plus lots of liquor (only Frenchmen drank wine). Scotch and rye were the drinks of choice. I never actually tried this one, because, one, I was underage; and two, I preferred my cornflakes with milk. But our neighbor did; he liked it so well, he stayed on it for the next 20 years, and he was a vegetarian.

What attracted me to Dr. Atkin's Diet Revolution was that he didn't count calories, and he didn't have a problem with protein or fat. So he would have been my man if he hadn't been so sticky about carbohydrates—I'm not big on pasta, but I do like my sweets, and the 20 grams one was allowed at the beginning of the Revolution didn't cut it for me. Once I realized I would have to lose my cookies, I decided to try the Boston Police Diet and Weight Containment Plan.

Again protein, my favorite, was in, but fruits and vegetables in any quantity were out. Chubby thumbs down on this one. If I was going to go with law enforcement, I preferred taking my orders from West Point. Their Fitness and Diet Plan was better because it not only allowed healthy (or unhealthy?) portions of meat and didn't particularly care how much fat was on them but it also offered a complete exercise regimen. So for one who, in 1977, was beginning to show signs of middle-age spread, I figured it wouldn't be bad having a cadet's physique. I tried it for a whole week, and when my measurements didn't budge and I didn't end up with a commission, I gave up.

Not being a smoker, I never tried the I Quit Smoking Diet, and I didn't even have a computer when Antonetti's Computer Diet Plan arrived on the scene, so *that* one was out, but there were enough others to keep me and my friends going. I knew all the intimate details (including the sordid tale of Jean Harris) about the Scarsdale Diet, the Stillman Diet, Dr. Solomon's High Health Diet, Dr. Cooper's Fabulous Fructose Diet, and of course in the later years, the Pritikin Principle Diet Plan. In addition to the Big Names, I eagerly devoured articles in women's magazines that told me how I could maintain my girlish figure into my nineties and beyond.

Then I stopped. Not because I couldn't lose weight on almost any diet I tried, but because I could. I dropped pounds eating *fewer* carbs and *more* fat, and I dropped pounds eating *more* carbs and *less* fat. I could lose weight by limiting my caloric intake to 1,000 calories or I could lose weight by not paying attention to calories at all. I also noticed, if I ate as much meat (and fat) as a Boston Policeman, I would be a nice, roly-poly, middle-aged woman, while my husband, fed the same meals, wouldn't gain an ounce. Just as a man I know, reasonably healthy for most of his adult life, enjoys a bowl of high-fat ice cream each night before going to bed and remains pencil thin at age 90. If I had even half a bowl of *nonfat* yogurt every night, I would be shopping for new clothes.

The sad truth is: some people can eat anything they want and not gain an ounce, while other people just look at a brownie and gain a pound. If you, as I, fall into the latter category, I have discovered what is probably the only fast and completely reliable way to lose those extra pounds. Step One: Weigh yourself holding a heavy object. Step Two: Drop it. You'll be amazed at how quickly the pounds just fall away.

ON THE GRANDKIDS

Oh, child of my child,
What natural selection
Has caused you to be
This pearl of perfection?

Yo, Grandma ... How About a Dell Axim X30?

If you find yourself wistfully thinking of the days when you could walk into a toy store and know what you were looking at (a Raggedy Ann is a Raggedy Ann is a Raggedy Ann), or you remember too well how easy it was to find (and pay for) those ever-popular, oh-so-familiar G.I. Joes and Barbies that used to top the little ones' lists, chances are your grandkids have just hit the double digits, and you, the coolest of grandparents, have never seen, heard of, or bought any of the gift suggestions on any of their lists.

Fast-forwarded into the mysterious world of technology, you're up the creek without a digital compass. There are only three things you know for sure: whatever the latest piece of equipment your girl or boy wants for Christmas, Hanukkah, or his or her birthday, is going to have both letters and numbers in its title; it will cost a lot of money; and you won't know what it is when you see it. *And* to buy it, you will have to go to an unfamiliar super-superstore with rap music blaring and display cases filled with enough electronic equipment to signal all the known planets in our universe and those yet to be discovered. Not to mention the final humiliation. Since you have no idea what you're buying, you are reduced to handing the salesman, who sweeps the hair out of his eyes, a slip of paper with the name carefully copied from your grandchild's list, letter for letter, number for number, because you're aware, the mere transposition of an *X* and a 3 and that MP3 player may totally be over. At this point you feel like a child in an old movie, being put on a train with a note to the conductor: "Take good care of Suzy Adams and see that she gets off at North Wiponski Falls."

The plus side to pushing this electronic envelope is, despite the spiraling costs involved (the bigger the grandchild, the bigger the price), you never have to worry about whether this grandchild or that already has a cell phone, a DVD player, a digital camera, because the Motorola MOTOKRZR K1 ($159.99) you gave last year will be oh-so-not "in" next year; and if you think an 8-megapixel camera ($199.99) is going to last forever, like from one Christmas to the next, you're in for sticker shock when you see what the 10-pluses are going for ($350 and up).

But not to worry. I have arrived at a near perfect solution for filling your grandchild's order without blowing your IRA. If it's the iPhone 3G ($299.99) she wants, don't fuss, buy it. But do as I do now that the kids' stomachs are as big as their eyes—be sure to enclose a card that reads:

To Josh (Sarah, Eliza, Matthew),

Merry Christmas, Happy Hanukkah, Have a Great Year

at School, Happy Birthday, and—oh, yes—all my love on St. Swithin's Day. I guess it's a little early for Best Wishes on Your Forthcoming Wedding.

Grandma Lyla (Blake Ward)

Advise and Resent

Swollen Tongue Syndrome: a condition caused by the frequent biting of one's tongue to keep from giving unsolicited child-raising advice to one's adult children.

Any grandmother today worth her running shoes knows honesty is not the best policy when dealing with one's children about *their* children. No matter how passionately or fervently you want to offer an opinion on anything, I say, "Suck it up." So what if little Tommy, who never goes to bed before eleven o'clock, sleepwalks through most of the day? Or if Jenny is chewing, with her full set of teeth including molars, on the pacifier she just picked up from the dirty floor? As soon as you feel a gasp coming on—maybe a sentence that begins with "Why don't you . . ."—take a deep breath, swallow hard, and bite your tongue. Better a swollen tongue than a daughter or son who revokes your babysitting privileges.

Newer grandmothers may make the mistake of thinking they're being asked for advice because a daughter or daughter-in-law says something that ends with a question mark like: "Boy, potty training is really tough, isn't it?" Understand, this is a rhetorical question, not the opening you've been waiting for. Do whatever you have to do. Clear your throat, bite your tongue, but under no circumstances answer, "It wouldn't be so hard if you hadn't waited until he was old enough to go to the Men's Room alone." No. No. And again no. What's called for here is a series of uh-huhs, nods of silent support, or, if you can manage it, a simple "Yes, it is!" *Gulp!*

Just to see if you get the idea, here's a multiple-choice quiz. Let's see how you do:

1. You have volunteered to pick your granddaughter up at the bus stop because your daughter, unexpectedly, has to work late. The morning forecast was for rain and temperatures in the low 60s. When little Peggy gets off the bus, shivering, wearing a sleeveless shirt, short-shorts, and open sandals, you . . .

(a) lace into your daughter about sending her daughter, your grandchild, to school wearing the equivalent of a bikini in subzero weather.

(b) casually mention the effects of chilling on the bones of an unusually thin child who doesn't eat anything.

(c) bite your tongue to keep from telling your daughter how appropriately *you* dressed *her* when *she* was Peggy's age.

2. You've planned dinner for six o'clock to accommodate your grandchildren's routine. At five o'clock your grandson announces he's hungry and wants some cookies. Your daughter says, "All right, but only two." You . . .

(a) suggest he have carrots or celery instead so that some of his meager appetite will be preserved.

(b) offer to pay for a course on parenting for your daughter and her husband.

(c) bite your tongue and try not to notice your grandchild leaving the dinner of "all his favorites" untouched on his plate.

If you answered *c* in both cases, you've been doing this for a while. If you answered *a* or *b*, you have a long way to go. What's good for your soul may not be good for your role.

The best relief for pent-up-advice syndrome is to talk to other grandmothers. Here you can say whatever you want. If *your* children made *their* children wear the slippers you bought them last Christmas when they walk on those cold tile floors, maybe they wouldn't have nasty coughs that hang on all winter. Or maybe if the kids didn't play soccer, basketball, hockey, football, *and* baseball, they might have some time left to do their homework. Or can you imagine what those pointy-toed shoes do to a 12-year-old's little feet? *Mmm.* That feels really good.

But the point here is to maintain a give-and-take relationship with your children. You give what they are willing to take. Young parents may demur at first when you offer to give up your own vacation to stay with the kids while your kids go off to the Caribbean for a week, but they're easily persuaded.

So you don't say everything that's on your mind! Big deal. Maybe you'll get lucky. Look what happened to me. Despite all the unorthodox, potentially ruinous methods my daughters used, and are using, to raise my grandchildren, somehow, some way, they're turning out to be terrific kids. Go know.

Pitcher Perfect

Who doesn't love to see her grandchild hit a home run or make a goal or guard against a slam dunk in the fifth-grade play-offs?

Most grandparents I know would travel east of the Mississippi if they lived west, or west if they lived east, to be there for the magic moment. And that's exactly what we do. We're off and running—okay, driving—to see our grandkids on the court, on the diamond, or on the field. Is it because we can't wait to see our favorite little action figures in action? Or is it more likely because we know that's the only way we'll ever get to see them?

These days not too many kids are going over the meadow and through the woods to Grandmother's house, at least during baseball, hockey, basketball, football, or soccer season, which pretty much means year-round. Games can be, and usually are, scheduled for Sundays, as well as Saturdays, Mother's Day, Father's Day. Not too many holidays are sacrosanct. If you're thinking of a family reunion, Christmas Day and New Year's Day may be your only options. Otherwise, any child signed up for a sport is expected to show up for every practice and every game as are their parents. And being out of the country is no excuse. They may be minors, but this is major league stuff.

As for dinner, day or night, how many hot dogs does it take to pump up a goalie? If Norman Rockwell were alive today, he would have to give up painting. Where would he find a whole family gathered around the table for a congenial Sunday dinner with Dad or Granddad carving the roast?

It's not only team members who sacrifice mealtimes; what self-respecting family is a no-show at their kid's game? Shouts of "Good job!" echo across the great field if a member on the blue team (sponsored by Sunshine Plumbing) stops a member on the red team (sponsored by H&C Bagel) from stealing second base. The excitement that reverberates through the makeshift grandstand is enough to knock an oldster off his place at the end of the bench, where he has been seated to accommodate his walker.

That's why it's the grandparents who are doing the traveling. After all, your schedules are not nearly as crowded as your grandchildren's. So if they can't go to your home? You go to theirs. And if your family is caught up in the sporting life, home is whatever field their child and your grandchild is playing on. The cost of the equipment needed to play all these games is considerable, but look at all the money saved on those Sunday roasts. And because they're always in uniform, children need fewer ordinary clothes.

Admittedly, my vision is not what it used to be. So when I look out at that field, there may be nine boys dressed in

Sunshine Plumbing blue, and I may not be able to make out his features, but I know and can say with assurance to the gray-haired lady sitting next to me, “That’s my grandson, Number Three.”

How Many Pixels Do *You* Have?

When my grandchildren were little, last year, I could read their holiday wish lists and more or less understand what I was being asked to buy. Even if I wasn't exactly sure what they did with PlayStation 1 or 2, I could walk into a store, spot it on a shelf, and, completely unaided, buy it.

This year? Forget it. Even the youngest of my relations has moved on to the higher levels of electronic equipment and left me in the dust. Isn't it enough I finally realized everyone I saw with a large disk in his or her ear was not profoundly deaf but sporting the accoutrement of an iPod? Apparently not, because I am now being asked to distinguish between that early "simple" music player (the "classic" iPod) and an 8- or 16-gigabyte iPod nano, which I can buy with either a HomeDock Deluxe or a SoundDock Digital Music System, unless I decide to buy a SanDisk Sansa e260 4GB MP3 Player with MicroSD Expansion Slot.

Or maybe it's a cell phone that tops the most-wanted list. A *cell phone*, not to be confused with the cell phone I carry in my bag to call 911 in case of an emergency. A *cell phone* suitable for gift giving has to have an MP3 player (whatever that is), FM transmitter, Bluetooth (I have a feeling this has nothing to do with incisors), a digital camera, and a video recorder. And I suppose you can also call home with it.

When my children, the parents of this youngest generation, were growing up, they and their friends sought to be preeminent in their collection of dolls or action figures, electric trains or baseball cards. Now it's megapixels. You show me your camera, and I'll show you mine. The old Kodak Brownie, once given to children when they reached 10 or 11, is now in the Heritage Museum, which would be fine with me if I could only understand what makes their successors tick—or, more appropriately, click. I vaguely understand what megapixels are all about. I guess image resolution has something to do with how clear a photo will be. But if you're just taking a picture of your friend eating ice cream, why do you need so many of them? And what about a 7X optical zoom, as opposed to a 5X optical zoom? Should I believe the salesman when he tells me bigger is better for my 9-year-old granddaughter?

What bothers me most is, I don't know what I'm buying. And as much as I'd like to keep my standing as a really cool grandma, when I walk into a store to make the purchase, I have to admit, I'm completely out of my elements.

Bragging Rights

Bragging is the inalienable right of grandparents. We get to tell all our friends how adorable, talented, brilliant, precocious the offspring of our offspring are because we earned it. Like our parents before us, no longer involved in the nitty-gritty details of actually *raising* the children, we are free to sing their praises to anyone and everyone whose hearing aid is in working order.

Free to sing, all right, but that doesn't mean anyone has to listen. Nothing clears a room faster than a sentence that begins, "Did I tell you about my grandson Jimmy (Peter, Paul, Prescott)?" So, Rule Number One: never come right out and say, "My grandson Jimmy is a genius. *Everybody* says so." You'll be talking into a dead mike. What you have to do if you want a friend, neighbor, or relative to know what a talented, gorgeous, and genetically advantaged grandchild you have is bring up the subject in a carefully planned, spontaneous manner. I, personally, have been very successful with the innocent photo technique. This is the one where you bring out a photo of Jimmy (or Alex or Casey or Roger) ostensibly to illustrate how much he's grown since your friend saw him last. And there he is, stretched to his full 48 inches, standing, it just so happens, in front of a huge banner that reads:

Fairbrook Middle School's
Most Outstanding Student Ever
James Ward

Next to it you may choose to place a large magnifying glass and say, "He *is* getting big, *isn't* he?"

If a suitable photo is not available, you can still work almost any conversation around to the point where you can slip in a subtle reference to your grandchild. On the surface, a discussion of the Middle East doesn't seem to offer too many possibilities. But listen:

Me: "I don't know what we're going to do in the Middle East. It's such a mess."

My cousin: "It is. I think one of the reasons we've had so much trouble in Muslim countries is we don't have enough people who speak Arabic."

[Opportunity!]

Me: "You're right. I was just saying that to our Suzy the other day. You know she's absolutely fluent in French. She has such a natural ear. I told her she should take Arabic if they offer it in fourth grade. But you know kids today: she's determined to learn Chinese."

The photos and conversation are good ploys, but probably the best way of boasting without boasting is to let your guests discover for themselves how talented Samantha (or Jenny or Clyde or Patsy) is with mosaics (or woodworking, painting, pottery, decoupage). Instead of your saying,

"I must show you the exquisite bowl Samantha made in her mosaics class," you simply arrange to place the bowl, along with the picture frame, the mirror, the candy dish, and the wall plaque, in strategic spots around the living room until it is alight with those tiny shiny tiles. Then you put the bowl—using as little fruit as possible and no doily, so the intricate mosaic design shows up in all its glory—in the middle of the bridge table and wait for the players to take their seats. At which point someone is sure to comment, "What a beautiful bowl. Where did you buy it?" And here's the opening: "Buy it? Oh, no. My granddaughter Samantha made it. Let me see . . . did I put out a few of the other things she made? Oh, yes, there's the vase, the picture frame, the mirror, the candy dish, and that's the wall plaque on the wall next to the photo of Jimmy."

You may wonder why I'm willing to share all my carefully developed techniques with others who may very well use them against me should we meet someday. Let's just say I've learned a lot in my 25 years of grandparenting, and I want to give new GPs a leg up. *And*, as my grandson Jeff, the humanitarian, said to me when he called from Nigeria, where he's working night and day, without pay, in sweltering heat, to stamp out infertility, "Grandma, I guess I'm just like you. I always want to help others."

A Working Relationship

I'm worried about my grandchildren finding jobs. Even before all the credit institutions began tanking, the economy was beginning to show signs of strain: people ordering wines from Qatar instead of Montepulciano, jeans by Levi's instead of Calvin Klein. So, because everyone else in the family is working hard just to keep a car in every garage, it has fallen on me, the grandmother with time on her gnarled hands, to think of new ways my grandchildren can put their $200,000 college educations to use. Listen, my children, and you shall hear what Granny has found are *the* jobs of the year. My exclusive picks include Political Strategist, Pundit, Spokesman. Eat your heart out, Craigslist.

As a news junkie of global proportions, I watch channels doing 24/7 news at least 12/7 of the time. What I've observed is, these all-news channels (CNN, MSNBC, FNC) are using up pundits and political strategists faster than they're being born. Some are being deployed four or five times a day. Even Pat Buchanan or Donna Brazile may have to powder their noses, and that's when those pundits-in-waiting whose grandmothers have been smart enough to give them a heads-up can jump in. "Here I am, Mr. Cable News Producer. Don't let my degree in nuclear physics fool you. I'm wired and ready to go."

That's one of the great things about these 21st-century jobs. One's résumé is never actually presented to the viewer. So if my granddaughter—to choose someone at random—was a reporter on her school newspaper, her introduction need only describe her as a journalist from South Bend, Indiana. Credits are not important. Opinions are. Take economics. Although this same granddaughter, whose experience in the workplace is limited, may not be fully conversant with the workings of the international banking system, she does know when help from home dries up, and what effect the credit crunch has on a middle-class family's clothes budget. So if all that is called for is a talking head, she certainly has one, and a pretty one at that.

Of course, the demand for political strategists has lessened somewhat since the election. Many among this unending stream of Democrat and Republican soothsayers now find themselves in an unemployed state (red or blue) of work, and since punditry is a natural segue from the more limited role of political strategist, a lot of them have gravitated toward this not-so-seasonal occupation. Only a skeleton crew has hung in there to immediately begin planning the 2010 reelection campaigns of those congressmen elected in 2008. But as I said to my family the other day, even if you have to start as an understudy for David Gergen or Gloria Borger, on the day either one comes down with laryngitis or hives, you'll be opinionated and ready to go.

Still, television is not for everyone. The granddaughter of a friend of mine, who is also looking for a job (but truthfully is not as good-looking as my Scarlett), would do well to consider becoming a spokesman—or, rather, a spokes*person*. This is a growing market, because hardly a day goes by that someone or some company has not been accused of something. And the beauty of it is, for the job seeker if not the accused, the more the indictments, the more the job opportunities. Banks and credit markets are failing. Stockholders are threatening to cut the strings on executives' golden parachutes. Government is looking into financial hanky-panky. This is not the time a CEO or CFO of a bankrupt enterprise wants to meet the press to explain why he authorized $440,000 and change for a sales junket shortly after being bailed out by the federal government. Better to have a spokesperson, anonymous and faceless (who would waste his flashbulbs on a nobody?) read a prepared statement and not be expected to take any questions.

With precise diction, one of the few requisites for this job (another being you have to be able to read), the SP can assure reporters huddled in a small anteroom next to the Executives' Health and Fitness Club, the only reason the company sponsored this outing was to motivate the executives to go all out to achieve the best possible bankruptcy terms. As for the price tag: not excessive. You can't serve cheap wine to people who have been drinking champagne at the company's expense for their entire careers *and* expect to keep their loyalty. We should also keep in mind, while all the attention has been focused on the investors whose life savings may have been washed away, they are not the only ones who have suffered. The company's executives, named in this indictment, will, in all probability, see their year-end bonuses reduced by millions.

Let's face it: the plushy days of full employment are behind us. This is a time for young job seekers (and their grandmothers) to make milk out of a cow's ear. If for some reason you can't be a political strategist, a pundit, or a spokesperson, other opportunities are all around you. Hundreds, if not thousands, of bankers are going to need help writing their résumés. More and more auctioneers will be needed to sell off the contents of hedge fund managers' estates. And how many used Ferrari salesmen are there?

Sure, there is a downside. Benefits given in these kinds of jobs are limited. It's unlikely you'll get health insurance or paid vacations. But look on the bright side: deductions from your paycheck will be minimal, and if you're really lucky, no one will offer you an IRA.

You're welcome.

ON TECHNOLOGY

I'm all for computers,
I'd never deride them,
My issue is with
Those demons inside them.

Computer Speak

Do you know what it feels like to have your computer tell you, flat-out, your cookies have been disabled? Let me tell you, it's pretty unsettling. First, to find out my cookies (whatever they are) are not working. And second, to realize someone out there knows more about my cookies than I do.

I don't claim to know how computers actually work, but I do know there is something creepy going on when I turn my computer off at night, no power, dead, and find an icon for Nero Express on the screen in the morning. I didn't ask for Nero Express. I don't even know what Nero Express is, so how did it get there? *Who's* been playing with *my* symbols?

Like most people these days, I lock the doors when I go to bed at night; the windows, too. That's worked pretty well so far to protect me and my family from human intruders. But what good does that do when an Unidentified Computer Object (UCO) can creep into my house undetected, in the dead of night, and leave unnerving messages on my machine: "An error was committed at 3:40 A.M." followed by " . #) ∂ % ! + = v Ω √ . 3:40 A.M.?" At 3:40 this morning, I was in bed, fast asleep. If someone committed an error at that ungodly hour, it certainly wasn't me. It's like seeing a call made to Nigeria on your phone bill when you've just learned the area code for Ohio.

So who was it? And what about the “. #) ∂ % ! + = v Ω √ . ?” Am I, whose only FBI experience has been gleaned from watching *Without a Trace*, supposed to break this code?

My old '65 Selectrix (may it rest in peace) only wrote what I told it to write. It didn't have any thoughts of its own. It had a ball of fonts, so, like the computer, you could change the typestyle at will, but it didn't suddenly, inexplicably change type size or print **bold** because it decided it was time for a change. When I turned off the power at night, the typewriter, like any normal machine, was out of business—dead. I never had to worry about what was going on under the covers.

Probably the eeriest message of all used to appear on the first Sunday in April. When I would wake up, there it was: “Your clock has been changed to daylight savings time.” On its own initiative, it switched my clock before I even had a chance to remind myself whether you spring or fall forward. A few years ago, when the time change was moved to the second Sunday in March, I ran to my computer to see if it had been tipped off, and there it was—the message from No One. Think of it: while I was four rooms away, blissfully asleep, a new time was already on my screen. Great for me, but how do computers in non-observant states like Arizona or Hawaii know where they live? And last year, when only certain counties in Indiana went through the changes, did their computers know which was which, or were there a few people late for work on Monday?

What really worries me is how vulnerable I am to computer rebuke. It's one thing to be warned about some vague error having occurred, or that I've committed an illegal act and my program is going to be shut down. But what if it decides to punish me because I've never used any of its wizards (in fact I've requested the too-eager paper clip to stop dancing), or I've ignored its advice on punctuation or spelling?

It may be time to pay the typer. My nightmare is, one day I will go to my machine and see the ultimate message on the screen: "You have a fatal personality flaw. We don't like you. Don't press any key. Your computer will never start again. .⊠) ∂ ⊠⊠ + = v Ω ⊠." Oh, well, I guess that's the way the cookies crumble.

Dot Not So Calm

If the online-shopping industry wants to continue growing, they're going to have to do it without me. I give up. It's not that I don't want to give them my business, I've visited so many dot-coms there's a blank on my keyboard where the period used to be. Even though I've never been in a store that asks you to sign in before you get so much as a peek at the merchandise, I do just what they tell me to. If they ask me to register, they've got it. I click "Register."

Obediently, I fill out each field. I accept their privacy code. Anything they want. I give them my user name. I enter in my password. I click "Submit." The little browser icon at the top of my screen goes round and round, checking me out. It doesn't like what it sees.

I'm instructed to try again. They say some part of my application was either inaccurate or incomplete. Which part is left to my imagination. Since I'm pretty sure of my name, address, and telephone number, that leaves my user name and/or password. I give it a few more tries. I know I have a list of passwords around here someplace, but this e-merchant doesn't like my answers. I give up on that site.

New try. Great. No need to register. They say I can just

browse the site. They welcome me. I'm feeling all warm and fuzzy, looking around for a few minutes, a *very* few minutes. I'm just about to order what I want when a message appears on the screen, telling me, in effect, that I've taken too long, there are other customers waiting. I can try again later. I've been bumped. A little discouraged but still game, I go to a site that's promising free shipping if I order by midnight. Fine. All the colorful boxes appear on my screen with the various categories and products offered. I click on my category. I wait. I wait, and I wait. My mouse is frozen. I press every button I can reach. Nothing works. I can't go on with my order. I can't escape.

Finally, the message appears: "HTTP error 403. 403.9 access forbidden. Too many users are connected."

Once more. I'd really like to use this easy shopping tool. I have no trouble getting on to the next site. It's very user-friendly. It likes me. This time there are no glitches. I find what I want in the color I want and the size I want, and I would have ordered it if a message in bold black lettering, with a verboten symbol on it, had not appeared on my screen.

"This program has performed an illegal operation and will be shut down." *Vavoom.* Is that a knock on the door? Who's to blame for this illegality—my computer or me? I've been taken off-line in shame.

The next day, still anxious to save all that time standing in line at a store, I sign on as usual and sit quietly as my connecting number is tried. It isn't busy. Good sign.

Everything's a go until Step Six. Connecting to AOL. The screen freezes. No movement at all. I wait, and I wait.

At last The Message appears: "The modem has lost the carrier signal. Please try signing on again later."

Not me, brother. You had your chance. These little fingers are going to do their walking in the Yellow Pages. I'm cyberspaced out.

Help Unwanted

What Microsoft Word doesn't seem to understand is, I'm not interested in what It has to say. I don't want an answer to questions I haven't asked. I don't want to explain my every move to a computer. I don't need or want a collaborator. Just fill in the spaces.

My old typewriter never talked to me. I typed, it printed. If it didn't approve of my dangling participles, run-on sentences, and bad grammar, I never heard about it. When I started using Word and saw little squiggly red lines under some of my words and little squiggly green ones underlining whole sentences or even paragraphs, I didn't know what to make of it. I typed in "Newtown (CT)," and the squiggles appeared. Word suggested I change it to "Newton." Isaac? MA? I spelled *judgment* without an *e* (Webster's first choice); Word suggested I change it to *judgement* with an *e*. We began having polite but persistent arguments over spelling and grammar. I couldn't ignore the squiggles, because if I had a real spelling error or an obvious grammatical boo-boo, I'd want to know about it. It's the advice I could live without.

Word doesn't like the one- or two-word sentences I use

for effect. Fine. (There goes the squiggle.) That's Its (squiggle) opinion. I don't like It finishing my sentences for me. I start writing the month, Word rushes in with the day and the year. Maybe I want to see if *I* knew the day and the year on my own. The other day I typed in "Dear M," and Word filled in "Mom and Dad." I'm a senior citizen for goodness' sakes. Mom and Dad?

Letter writing is the worst. I have no sooner put in the date, with or without Its help, than that perky little box appears on the right side of my screen. At the bottom is a perky little dog with a wagging tail, who apparently is doing the talking, though I'm pretty sure none of this is his idea. He says:

> It looks like you're writing a letter. (None of your business.)
> Would you like help? (Not from you, Fido.)
> [*And here are my options:*]
> - Get help with writing the letter.
> - Just type the letter without help.
> - Cancel. (With pleasure.)

Why can't this pup understand, once and for all, I want to write my letters myself?

No doubt, Word has some admirable qualities and spares writers some embarrassing mistakes. But James Joyce's stream of consciousness would have driven It wild, and imagine what Word would have suggested to Dr. Seuss. That name? Forget it. How about Dr. Sues, See, Seas, Zeus, Sets, or Sews. And those books! What nonsense to write:

"There's a wocket in my pocket." Word thinks it should be "There's a wicket in my pocket," or a "docket," "rocket," or "socket." *How the Grinch Stole Christmas*? That'll never fly. Word has a better title: *How the Grenache Stole Christmas*, or *the Granite, Grant, Grunt,* or *Grantee*. Think of the "success" Dr. Seuss would have had if only he had paid more attention to grammar.

And what about the Gettysburg Address? We consider it one of the greatest speeches in American history. What would Word have suggested to Mr. Lincoln? To find out, I typed in the last section of the Address:

> It is rather for us to be here dedicated to the great task remaining before us—that from these honored dead we take increased devotion to that cause for which they gave the last full measure of devotion—that we here highly resolve that these dead shall not have died in vain—that this nation, under God, shall have a new birth of freedom—and that government of the people, by the people, for the people, shall not perish from the earth.

It was entirely underlined with squiggles, and Word had only this to say: "Long sentence (no suggestion)." I rest my case.

Me and My GPS

A few weeks ago I became the proud owner of a GPS unit. For those of you who are less cool than I, that's short for "global positioning system," which means, in effect, put me and my car down anywhere—Biloxi, Mississippi, or Trenton, New Jersey—give me the street address, and *vavoom!* We're there. No stopping at a local gas station, dry cleaner, or pet shop to ask directions. No hassling about whether I was supposed to turn left or right at the third intersection after the fourth traffic light. All I have to do is rest my foot on the gas pedal and listen to the mellifluous tones of The Lady inside my navigational system, who, with no malice aforethought, tells me where to go.

Because I've had my device only a short time, The Lady and I are just getting acquainted. But no doubt about it, she's a take-charge gal. Amazing, really. All I have to do is look at the small screen (which is not unlike the one on my BlackBerry, cell phone, iPod, or handheld Boggle) and touch the picture of a map that says "Show Map" under it, or a house ("Address"), or a map with a pin stuck in it ("Points of Interest"), and she does the rest.

For our first outing, I chose "Address" and, at her

direction, began touching the letters of my destination city: East Haddam. I pushed *E*; she said "E." I pushed *A*; she said "A." I pushed *S*; she said "S." I pushed *T*; she said "T." I pushed *H*; she said "H." I pushed *A*; she said nothing.

I tried again and again, but The Lady wouldn't let me finish. No way would she allow me to enter my *D*. I can't be sure what she had against East Haddam, but she gave me only two choices: Eastham or Easthampton, both in Massachusetts and neither of which had a regional theater I'd ever heard of, and they certainly weren't holding matinee tickets for my husband and me. Through perseverance—and no help from the manual, which seemed not to have any precedent for my problem—I finally figured out that it was the "East" she didn't like. So I punched in *H-A-D-D-A-M* by itself, and we were on our way.

Maybe not exactly the way I would have chosen, though. She couldn't have known about the construction on Route 7 near our house, or she wouldn't have tried so desperately to make me take that road.

I had to override her command, which apparently ruffled her feathers, because her voice went up at least two decibels. "Recalculate. Recalculate," she practically shouted, as if I were about to go over a cliff.

Every time I took an unauthorized turn, she tried to get me back on her road, and even though she was laying a guilt trip on me ("Why did she buy me if she wasn't going to use me?" I could imagine her thinking), I couldn't give in, because I was the one in traffic and she was the one all snugly inside that little 14-ounce wonder.

Finally, I did reach the main route, and when I turned

left, as she instructed, I could practically hear her sigh of relief. "Drive nineteen-point-two miles on I-Ninety-Five," she said contentedly. When it was almost time to get off the Interstate, she announced, "Point-five miles to Exit Sixty-Four." Then, "Turn right on Exit Sixty-Four. Turn left at the foot of the ramp." And so the directions went until I arrived at my destination—within two minutes of the estimated time.

Since then, The Lady and I have made several trips together, and I have nothing but admiration for the system and its spokesperson. At times, she may offer a little more information than I feel is necessary. For instance, did you know there's a Westport not only in Connecticut but also in Massachusetts, Maine, New York, Missouri, Kentucky, Washington, California, Indiana, Pennsylvania, South Dakota, Oklahoma, and Tennessee?

But that's a small price to pay for never again having to look for a red mailbox next to a crumbling stone pillar on a dark country road where you've been sent to pick up a fourth for bridge. And although there have been a few bumps along the way, my GPS unit and I are an item and, quite frankly, at this point I'm not ashamed to say, I'd be lost without her.

Digital Reality

The first time I saw someone using his thumbs to input a message on his BlackBerry, I couldn't believe it. First I thought, maybe he only has thumbs, but no, there were four other digits attached to each hand. Then why, given any finger, would he choose his thumbs? And the bigger question: how was he able to fit their bulky little bodies on the tiny letters and numbers of the handheld device?

Since then, I have seen these sturdy little benders pressed into service not only on BlackBerries, but on Treos, iPhones, and even the teensiest of cell phones. Amazing, because as we all know, thumbs have traditionally been looked down on, and not just by the other fingers. Maybe because they rhyme with *bums*, and loosely with *clumsy*, they've had an image problem. Society has never viewed thumb suckers in a positive light, and "thumbing a ride" is not way up there as a means of transportation.

Call me a finger snob, because if I had seen someone using his pinkies, I wouldn't have given it a second thought. Pinkies are adorable. They're the universal darlings of our hands. And, as the designated piggies that ran *all* the way home, they've tickled little children through the ages. In addition, a pinkie elevated, while holding a teacup, is an official sign of breeding.

The index finger would have been a predictable choice. It is indisputably utilitarian and generally well regarded. Those old enough to remember dial phones are intimately acquainted with this digit, and even today, it is frequently employed in pointing and turning pages.

The fourth finger, just a hair taller than the index, has come on hard times, so this choice might have been a little iffy. It's dropped in status due to the fact it has lost its exclusive right to be called the ring finger. While still the official bearer of engagement and wedding rings, today's styles allow for the wearing of rings on *all* fingers; all but the thumb, which is, to its further denigration, seldom adorned.

The middle finger, by reason of its size (it's the tallest), has the necessary stature. It might have been a good choice except it is not designed to work alone. It is usually used in conjunction with other fingers, such as in making a fist, waving, or shaking hands. When used on its own, to its embarrassment, it creates a less than polite gesture.

So how come the thumb, rather than the index finger, say, was chosen to be the head honcho of the small electronics world? Well, the story goes, a Canadian techie hired to test text the newly developed BlackBerry broke his index finger, rendering it immovable. His finger in a splint, desperate to keep his job, he was forced to try another finger. The pinkie, as noted, was cute but useless; the ring and middle—tall but weak. So by default, the job went to the midget digits. His hopes hung on his thumbs, and they didn't let him down.

However, this version is bitterly disputed by the influential Jack Horner Foundation of the U.S. and Canada, which claims, without prejudice, their thumbprints are all over it.

Whatever.

The Password Is ... Forget It

I've just about had it with passwords. Why does my bank need more assurance that I'm me? They already have my "secret" PIN number (we both know what my "xxxx" stands for), and once I've contacted them online, they know my e-mail address, so do we really need all this cloak-and-dagger stuff?

Someone up there in Programmer Land must have been frightened by an old gangster movie: Jimmy Cagney knocks on the door of a speakeasy, and before the goon doorman will let him in, Cagney, a.k.a. Bugsy, has to give a password to prove he's not a dirty rat or a copper. We know those guys were hiding illegal booze or floating crap games. But what's eBay up to? Why do I need a password to view the bidding? Is their merchandise hot, or are they afraid that vintage waffle iron is going to fall into the wrong hands?

Listen up, fellas. Prohibition is history, not even so modern anymore, and state-sponsored gambling pays for some of our schools, so one has to wonder why, if I don't remember "Doodle 3" (not my real password), I pose a threat to American Express. Maybe I'm going to steal secret travel plans or make off with some incredible reward or benefit. Oooh, ooh, they're scared.

Even the post office, our own semi-government agency, which could check the Social Security number I plug in against the one in that big cyberspace file in the sky, asks me to create a password before it will allow me to order stamps online. *And* they have very definite ideas of what kind of password it should be: a minimum of eight letters, at least one uppercase, one lowercase, and one numeral. Got that? It took me four tries. First I forgot the uppercase, then the lowercase, and then the numeral completely slipped my mind. When I finally gave them what they wanted and was asked to retype it to verify the password was really mine, I put in the wrong numeral, and the silent sirens went off. Stop that impostor. She can't even retype her password. No stamps for her.

It would still be ridiculous, but not as bad, if we could use one password for everybody, but that's just a pipe dream. So I've come up with a solution I think would satisfy all parties: a national registry of passwords, something like Social Security numbers, safe and protected from identity thieves. And now that the Democrats have control of the House, a few thousand workers can probably be hired to man the newly created Bureau Underwriting Letters and Ledgers for Safe Holding. The result? When you or I want to enter a chosen site and are asked for a password, we would just have to type in B-U-L-L-S-H . . . and before we can be asked if we want to continue running script on the page, we're in.

ON THE PAST (PERFECT)

The older you get,
The more the perception
That everything past
Was utter perfection.

Mother Is the Invention of Necessity

I don't know what all the fuss is about these days. Handling girls from ages 13 through 19 doesn't have to be a nightmare. Take it from one who's been there and done that. I'm not saying I was the perfect mother, just almost, but when my daughters were teenagers, we got along like three fingers of the same glove. Someone may have wiggled every so often, but no one got too far out of hand. How did I do it?

First, I never spoke until I was spoken to, and even then I didn't say much. Each daughter knew that her long moody silences would not be interrupted by a cheery voice. When she did speak, even if it was only once a week, the time and topic were hers. She may have wanted to discuss deeply what time dinner would be ready, maybe even what we were having for dinner—if she was feeling particularly expansive. I tried to treat these subjects as I did sex information when she was very young: I never told her more than she wanted to know. I knew instinctively while it's all right to say, "We're having roast beef, salad, and fruit," it's *not* all right to add, "Do you think you should be eating a whole bag of chips right before dinner?" This would be offensive on two counts. One, it violated her civil liberties by suggesting she does not have the right to ruin her own appetite; two, it's a question.

Anyone who's ever had a teenager in the house for more than two weeks knows things must never be put into the form of a question. I hadn't learned this with my first daughter. I used to ask her, "What grade did you get in algebra?" or "What time will you be home?" or "What is Moose's last name?"—never realizing such questions were a flagrant invasion of privacy. After much slamming of doors and music turned up to infinite decibels, I finally got the picture. Short statements are allowable; prying questions are not.

This didn't mean I never had a chance to speak my mind. I certainly did. I can't count the times one or the other of my daughters knocked on my bedroom door, fairly begging for my opinion—how did I feel about a girl wearing the same dress to two consecutive dances?—or desperate to know, did I think my blue shirt would go well with *her* blue shorts? Or which did I think was better: a party for 50 kids in the summer or an indoor winter blast? Actually, I was in on all their innermost thoughts. About the only things we didn't discuss were religion, politics, morals, and other superficialities.

I know how open our communication lines were because the girls not only came to me for advice (see above) but also felt free to give me the benefit of theirs. Not every mother's daughters care enough to tell her when she's wearing her skirts too short (or long), or choosing a lipstick too bright (or dull) for her complexion, or using the wrong makeup to hide her wrinkles. Mine were thoughtful enough to vote on my hairstyles, personally supervise my wardrobe, and keep me informed on opportunities for my self-improvement.

Their fashions, however, were on the Most Unwanted Conversation list. I learned not to flinch when I saw one of our budding young women dressed modishly in elephant-leg pants, an Indian jacket, and a floppy hat. (It was the sixties.) Doesn't every mother's heart swell at the sight of her daughter walking barefoot, hair hanging like so many assorted strings down her back? I told myself, I think the look is great. I do. I do. I do.

At the root of our communications was honesty. I never lied to the girls. I never tried to tell them I was young once. Why lose their confidence? They knew, and I was taught to know, I was born at the same time they were; only I was already gray and set in my ways. Otherwise I would realize that 13-year-olds go steady; eye makeup is permissible, even mandatory, in seventh grade; separate-but-equal facilities (including telephone, hair dryer, and maid service) are the birthright of each family member; a girl of 16 is perfectly capable of driving cross-country chaperoned by another girl of 16. I would know all this if only I had had the chance of being young once.

The most wonderful thing about this planned motherhood was the relationship that developed between my daughters and me. I was entirely reciprocal. They knew they could talk, I knew I could listen. They knew they could question, I knew I could answer. They were confident of my unwavering support—and I was sure of it too. There was absolutely nothing *I* wouldn't do for each other.

The proof of our rare understanding was epitomized when my older daughter and I negotiated to see how often *I* would be allowed to use *my* car. I cited my somewhat frivolous needs: going to work, grocery shopping, dental appointments, dry-cleaning, laundry, etc. She had more urgent ones: basketball games, avoiding the school bus, meeting friends. We couldn't seem to find a solution to the problem until my daughter, with that crystal clear thinking so characteristic of the young, observed, "You know, Mom, we just can't go on like this. We're not getting anywhere. So I was wondering, have you and Dad considered carpooling?"

Packing It In

I am a world-class packer. This isn't a boast. It's a fact. From long years of experience, I know when to roll and when to lay flat. I put tissue paper between dark and light colors. I stuff socks in empty corners. I know all about packing my clothes so they look freshly pressed when they come *out* of the suitcase. What I don't know is what to put *in* the suitcase.

It's not as if I'm lacking in the research department. As soon as I know where we're going, I visit Yahoo! Travel to find out the kind of weather we're likely to encounter: Vancouver. Average daytime temperature of 65 degrees in September. Looking past the numbers to the little picture on the screen, I try to make out what the tourists are wearing, aside from their happy smiles. That's when I start to obsess. Is that a denim jacket the woman has on? No, it looks heavier. Leather? Suede? What month were they there? It doesn't say. I have a leather jacket, but it's awfully heavy to pack, and I'm already carrying a lined raincoat, though I'm not sure I need the lining in September.

No need to call in the shrinks. I know what's wrong with me. I have a classic case of clothes anxiety, and even

I know where I got it. No, it wasn't my mother this time. It was my honeymoon that did it. My husband and I were married in early March. We chose Bermuda for our wedding trip. Picture Bermuda shorts, pastel shirts, lacy sweaters protecting against the soft tropical breeze.

Now picture a suitcase (part of a matched set) full of summer clothes and the thermometer straining to reach 50 while a frosty mist settles on the rosy coral beaches. Maybe if I had done the appropriate due diligence, I would have noticed Bermuda's peak season starts in mid-April and goes through June, so our weather was not as unseasonable as everyone at the hotel would have us believe. Luckily, I had brought along a yellow, full-length wool coat, just in case there was a cool night, and this afterthought never left my back for the 10 days we were there. Would you like to see my photo album? Umpteen years later, I still bear the scars of this early marriage trauma.

Seasoned travelers suggest layering[1] as the answer to keeping warm and cuddly when the temperature suddenly dips to an all-time low. Or, if the temperature starts to resemble a bad golf score, you can *un*layer, from jacket to shirt and so on, as modesty permits. However, this only works for the top part of your body. If you were to wear two pairs of pants you would look like Mr. Donut, and for me, wearing a pair of pants with a skirt over it would remind me of how my mother wanted me to go to school on cold winter days.

Besides, truth be known, mine is more than a weight

1 Layering occurs when you wear a jacket on top of a sweater, on top of a blouse, on top of a silk undershirt.

problem. The question of which blouse, which skirt, and which jacket to take becomes more and more nerve-racking as T-time approaches. And we're not talking crumpets here.

I have a friend who travels only with beige and black; everything is interchangeable: accessories, shoes, and bags can be kept to a minimum. Great idea, but because I've been foolishly buying pink, blue, brown, green, red, to name a few colors in my wardrobe, and assorted blouses, jackets, shoes, and bags to match, if I limited myself to only two shades, even interchanging them, I wouldn't have enough clothes for more than a two-day vacation. And if I got a spot on my one blouse, I'd have to go home.

So, to counter this problem, I tend to take a few more clothes than my friend. Maybe eight or ten more tops: short-sleeved, long-sleeved, and three-quarters are always nice. Three or four extra pairs of slacks (they tend to get so wrinkled), a short and a long raincoat (light or driving rain), cardigans, and pullovers. And before I realize my closet is empty, I'm into my supersize *40-inch* suitcase on wheels, the one I swore I'd never take again because it takes three people to lift it off the carousel at the airport.

While I'm packing, each time I tell myself I'm cured. Remember the last trip? I ask sternly. Not only weren't there enough hangers in the cabin (the room, the stateroom, the hotel), but because I had so many choices I would stand in front of the closet for 15 minutes, trying to decide the best outfit to wear for a salmon bake next to a river, where the fish were swimming upstream to their doom. Black, of course, but will I need a sweater? Cotton?

Wool? And what kind of hiking boots? My L.L. Beans (mid-calf, lined, water-resistant)? Or my Lands' Ends (short, leather, grip soles, perfect for mountain climbing)? Are there mountains between the boat and the river? The brochure is vague.

Just because I haven't been successful so far in controlling my take-everything-in-sight impulse doesn't mean I've given up hope for an ultimate cure. Call me a dreamer, but I'm looking forward to the day the first packing inhibitors hit the market. From then on I will pop one or two Valiseums[2] (prescription strength), pull out my 26-inch bag and, feeling as relaxed as someone who doesn't know she has four pairs of jeans to choose from, begin to pack for my trip.

2 Patent pending

The Saving Grace

I've always wanted to be the kind of person who comes home from a trip, takes her film to be developed, and as soon as she brings the prints home, pastes them in an album. And as long as I'm dreaming, labels each page—no, every photo on every page.

As it turns out, I'm not that kind of person. Not by a long shot. I'm a cross between a saver and a procrastinator—a victim of Paper Acquisition Disorder, commonly known as PAD. It's not that I don't *want* to throw out anything, it's simply that I *can't*. Unfortunately, this tendency pretty much disqualifies me for the housekeeper-of-the-year award, any year.

Still, I'm not a messy person. You don't trip over old newspapers when you walk into my house. Scenic shots, invitations, clippings, my children's third-grade report cards (they have children of their own now), restaurant reviews, filled notebooks are not just scattered about. They are stacked, bundled, clipped, banded. Except for my looseleaf notebook of recipes (more *loose* than leaf), where osso bucos wait patiently next to decadent chocolate cakes, sometimes for years, in hopes of a permanent page assignment.

Life is hard on PADers. Like everybody else, as we try new things, we acquire things, then more and more things—mementos that become tangible memories of places we've been, people we've seen. I have empty scrapbooks, *many* empty scrapbooks, fairly begging to have a saved Metro pass or a train schedule placed beneath their acetate sheets. But I also have in baskets, shoe boxes, envelopes, file folders, brimming over with dance recital programs, preschool artwork, birthday cards *with* their envelopes, noteworthy articles that will someday be valuable for something, unused bumper stickers, not to mention vestiges of our travels. How does one part with a 1982 Marriott Courtyard bill, passports three renewals old, ticket stubs from the Botanical Garden in Halifax, a city map of downtown Newark? If I committed one sin by forgetting to mail postcards from Mexico, should I compound it by just tossing them out, or save the glossy photos, usually better than the ones I took, for that colorful scrapbook I'm going to label "Our Trips"?

My husband dismisses my squirrel-like tendencies with an offhand "My wife saves everything!" That's absolutely not true. What he never seems to notice is, like many others, I do try to thin out. I limit myself to one year's worth of privacy notices, those little enclosures that come with your bank statement or department store bill; I go through my coupons at least every two years and discard those that expired two years ago. My shopping bag collection is formidable, but I don't save just any big old bag, I only keep those with rope handles or those from stores that are off my beaten path—way off, like Tiffany,

Gucci, Harrods. Only at Christmastime, when I need large bags to transport presents, do I save extras of the Big Brown Bag, Banana Republic, Gap, or Trader Joe's. I am, however, a pushover for minis and have more than my share of adorable little totes that must have cost the stores a bundle.

In some ways, I view myself as an unpaid historian. If I don't save business cards of people who are no longer in business, who will? Old magazines? What do you need? Stationery with our previous address on it? How many sheets? Calendars? What year? I figure I'm doing my bit for posterity by hanging on to furniture bills, guarantees, and instruction manuals. Future generations may one day be bidding on my GE washing machine installation diagram, aught four.

Storage, however, is a problem. We PAD people need room. We can't be contained. We must always live in houses with attics or walk-in closets; basements or crawl spaces are notorious for mildew. Desks can only hold so much, and unfortunately, you do have to be able to eat dinner at the dining room table. On the plus side, the storage space doesn't actually have to be accessible. It's not as if I'll ever have to get my hands on something quickly. These are not official records. (My husband has the deed to our house and the bills of sale to our current cars in a neat little accordion file someplace.) My savings can be on high shelves, in the garage, or in the toolshed, because as far as I'm concerned, they've all found their final resting places.

And speaking of resting places, I'm so proud of my family. Whenever we discuss the disposition of my worldly goods, no one is selfish or greedy. To the contrary, each one in turn has said:

"You take it."

"No, you take it."

"I wouldn't think of it."

They make me glad I saved all of their baby teeth . . . somewhere.

As Thyme Goes By

If I should live to one hundred and three,
And cook and bake continuously,
I'd barely tap that vast supply
Of recipes I've clipped to try.

My name is Lyla, and I am a recipe junky. For 50 years, I have been collecting recipes. I can't stop. If I'm in a dentist's office looking through magazines and there's a recipe for wilted spinach and graham crackers, I look for a copying machine. If I hear a recipe for kangaroo soup on my car radio, I jot it down on the nearest piece of paper: my registration, the owner's manual, whatever. I have to have it. Meats, Fish, Cakes, Salads, Sunday Suppers, Bar-B-Qs are all yellowing in accordion files, notebooks, albums, file boxes, and folders, just waiting to be tried.

If writing a cookbook held any promise (how does senior noncelebrity grab you?), I would be strongly tempted to scoop up a thousand or so of the best and publish a giant cookbook, *Lyla's All-Time Favorites*. Although nobody may know who I am, we could skirt that issue by hinting that I, too, got my start in Alice Water's kitchen at Chez Panisse. That way, the cookbook-buying public might think they *should* know who I am, and the book might sell a few copies. At the very least I would have a thousand fewer pieces of paper to deal with.

The problem with being a compulsive clipper is, having *one* recipe for Lady Baltimore Cake (which I don't even happen to like) or *one* recipe for Tuna Fish Casserole doesn't cut it. I need more and more. A Zesty Tuna Fish Casserole may have different ingredients from a Sunday Night Tuna Casserole—a dash of curry, perhaps a can of pimentos to spice up the sauce. A third one—for example, a Saturday Night Tuna Casserole for Company—may have no sauce at all, just a simple crusty layer of fresh bread crumbs that have been soaked in milk and wrung out. Yum.

Before the 1980s, recipes more or less knew their place, and that place was mainly in women's magazines. Each month I would flip through the pages and cut out a recipe for Banana Flambée here or a different version of Banana Flambée there, but my cutting was limited to a few hours a month. And if I remember correctly, I was still on my first accordion folder.

Then things took a turn for the worse. Recipes began popping up everywhere. And I had to have them all. If I found one on the side of a box, I cut it out with a razor, sometimes with disastrous effects for the crackers or the sugar inside. Home magazines that used to feature only kitchens, and the utensils and appliances you found in them, now had recipes for what you would cook in those kitchens with those utensils and appliances. Gardening articles not only told you how to grow vegetables but how to cook them after you'd grown them. Every grocery product began to offer a recipe book—*A Hundred Different Ways of Using Rigatoni*, or the like.

By the time the nineties arrived, I was out of my accordion, had two plump albums, two folders, and had just acquired a second file box. Now mail-order catalogs offered paella pans *and* a recipe for paella. Wellness newsletters had wellness recipes; restaurants on request would provide you with recipes for their specialties (secure in the knowledge no amateur chef was ever going to make his own Pickled Sharks' Fins or Steamed Bangladeshi Beef). At the fish market, if you bought fish, you got a recipe to go with it. At the supermarket, cooking demonstrations were ongoing and recipes handed out along with the samples.

And this was just in print. Enter the television chefs, either on their own programs or segments of morning shows. Because the ingredients were normally displayed on the screen as I was having my breakfast, most of these recipes are written either on the margin of the morning paper or on my shopping list for the day. I always promised myself I would copy them onto nice "From the kitchen of" recipe cards, but I've been busy for the past decade or so.

Even so, I was still getting by until, in what seemed like a flash, Web sites featuring recipes began to appear. The Internet was and is my final nemesis. Do you know how many recipes there are on the Internet? I don't, but I do know my printer is going as steadily as if I were printing my own daily newspaper. Now I no longer have to make hasty notes on the back of a pin as a television cook talks. I can simply go on the Web and print out the recipe, complete with method of preparation *and* a picture of the smiling chef holding the final product. I go through a lot of ink cartridges.

I've been asked when I think I'm going to make all these recipes. Such a foolish question. Does everybody who collects teapots drink tea out of each and every one of them? And who's using his snuffboxes these days? Besides, my collection provides me with a certain sense of security. I know, at any given moment, if anyone, anywhere, asks me for a recipe for meat chili, chicken chili, or vegetarian chili, I have two or three dozen I can print out at any time. As a matter of fact, if anyone reading this article is interested in a new way of preparing ostrich, just call me. My number is 1-800-NUTCASE.

This Little Twiggy Went to Market

The commercials have it right: At a certain age, a woman's skin *does* dry out. This happened to me when, still in my thirties, I saw what looked like driven snow flaking onto my shoulders. A friend of mine, who had already experienced such flaking, suggested I go to the store to buy some moisturizer that would rejuvenate my aging skin. Throwing my youngest child in her stroller, I went that very day.

At the cosmetics counter, I asked a saleswoman for help. I meant in choosing a moisturizer. She thought I meant in general. So after producing a tiny jar that was going to replace meat in my budget for a month, she could hardly keep the disdain and pity from her voice when she asked, "Would you like something for your eyes?"

I wasn't sure what she had in mind. A handkerchief? An eye patch? While I was weighing my choices, she whipped out a little plastic box with somebody's long curvy lashes inside. My first thought was, some poor woman, somewhere, is walking around without her eyelashes. Then I saw the others lined up in tiny cases on the counter: "long spikeys," "twisted fringes," and "demi-fulls," in prices from the ridiculous to the outrageous (I hoped my family wouldn't notice I was wearing the roast beef). Wrestling with myself, I looked in the mirror and saw two deep-set pools of brown sitting in the middle of a few lashes strung haphazardly on my lids. I was realistic enough to know that unless for some reason I said, "Look into my eyes," nobody ever did. And approaching 40, I was having a midlife crisis (or in current terms a quarter-life crisis). So leaving reason behind, I decided to go for it.

With a small crowd in attendance, the cosmetician worked me over. Within five minutes, my eyes were lined with soft black, my eyelids glowed with a mushroom brown shadow, and next to my own eyelashes were an unknown donor's long, curvy "natural fulls." I looked in the hand mirror, and Sophia Loren looked back. I hoped our friends would not see me as a threat to their homes, but I needn't have worried.

My new look lasted until bedtime, when I removed the lashes and put them back in their little box. I should never have taken them off. The next day, determined to wear them to the PTA meeting so that my coworkers would see what a Ways and Means chairman *could* look like, I tried putting them on.

The cosmetician, as I remembered, simply whisked them on. She had probably had a two-year training course. I had only an illustrated booklet. I did just what it told me to do, but the lashes refused to leave my fingers. Finally, after several unsuccessful attempts, I managed to get more glue on my eyelids than on my hands, and the lashes threw in the towel, so to speak. I was glamorous again.

At least temporarily, because all that glue I had spread

around did more than attach my false eyelashes. It attached all my eyelashes—to each other. Now, every time I closed my eyes in the course of an ordinary blink, my lids stayed down. When I stood at the meeting to give my report, I suddenly realized I couldn't see the president. She could see me, though, and several times asked if something was the matter. I said no and struggled on, opening my eyes whenever I could and keeping them closed whenever I couldn't.

Later, I decided having both eyes stuck together wasn't all that bad. One at a time was worse. During the coffee hour that followed, I would be talking to someone and find myself engaged in a long, involuntary wink. No sooner was I able to pry one eye open when—*wham*—the other one went down. Try explaining that to the principal of your daughter's junior high school. "I don't love you; it's just that my eyes stick shut," and then rush to pry them open before he's left his wife for you.

I made a lot of new friends that night, but I also developed the glue neurosis so common among beginning false eyelash users. If I used too much adhesive, I'd need a seeing-eye dog. If I used too little, I was in constant danger of losing my looks. Because these eyelashes *can* fall off. Not one at a time like your own do, where you cover the lash with your hand and make a wish. No. False eyelashes fall off all together when you're not thinking about it. And never at home.

My first experience with lash loss was at a dinner party. I turned from the person on my right, whom I thought had been looking so hard at me because I was a brilliant conversationalist, and scooped up a spoonful of soup. When I looked in the bowl, there, floating on top with the parsley, was my right eyelash. I didn't know what to do. I couldn't just slap it back on, fresh out of the soup, without at least getting rid of the parsley. On the other hand, allowing it to dry on the table wouldn't work either. I fished it out of the soup as unobtrusively as possible, wrapped it in a napkin, and excused myself as gracefully as I could.

Once in the powder room, I found I'd made another beginner's error. I hadn't brought my glue. Even the most thoughtful hostess, those who fill a little drawer in the guest bathroom with emery boards, hand cream, and deodorant, rarely provide glue for their guests. I was forced to return to the table, minus both my lashes and a good portion of my self-esteem.

As I became more proficient in the care and handling of eyelashes, I found too little glue was not the only reason lashes might fall off. Moisture, in any form, may cause either a curling up at the corners or complete loss. One of the worst things that can happen is a sudden rainstorm. Despite the fact that the tub of glue proclaims it to be a waterproof surgical adhesive, I found that when water hit my eyes, whether it be rain or tears, off came the lashes. In fact, because the adhesive is described as "surgical" and obviously doesn't work on me, I considered carrying an in-case-of-emergency card:

To whom it may concern:

In case of surgery, this patient will not stay together with glue.

The funny thing is, however, when you really *want* to remove the glue, at night before laying the lashes to rest, you can't get it off. Sometimes, I had to spend 15 or 20 minutes trying to peel all the adhesive away from the lash base, so I could get off to a clean start in the morning. At times like that, my husband, who actually enjoyed my new face (once I had gotten him to notice my lashes by batting them so unmercifully he kept looking for an open window), would get a little testy. At two or three in the morning, if he asked, "When are you coming to bed?" and I answered, "As soon as I take off my glue," he began to long for the old days, when I was not so "gorgeous," and he was not so tired.

Still, despite the high cost of beauty and the few sticky (and nonsticky) experiences I had, my lashes were a smashing success. In fact my "uppers" created such a stir, I would seriously have considered investing in "lowers," except I couldn't risk increasing my "batting average," because my husband kept complaining of the draft.

Sitting Pretty

It's easy to be athletic. What's hard is keeping your seat when all around you are jumping up to play eight sets of tennis or slalom down Mount Olympus. I found when we moved to the suburbs in the late fifties, my background in jump rope ("A! My name is Alice, and I come from Alabama!"), learned on the sidewalks of New York, would not cut it with our new friends and neighbors who all seemed to have teethed on tennis rackets and golf balls. With this crowd, it was clear from the beginning: it wasn't enough to be beautiful and sexy, and run your own business; you had to be able to drop one ski in the water, too.

Sports fever ran so high in the community, I knew I would have to shade the truth just a tad. If I was totally honest and said, "No, I don't play," when someone asked me to join her in a set of tennis or, "Sorry, I don't ski," if friends invited me on a ski weekend, my goose would have been cooked and I would have eaten alone. What I had to do was make everybody *think* I was great—at someone else's activity. I had to convince the tennis players I shot below par in golf and the golf players I was warming up for Wimbledon.

An important part of my scheme was to always dress

for the part or, more accurately, the part*s*. And I could have used a little more help from my husband, whose favorite outdoor sport turned out to be gardening. What's more, it was his loudly and often-expressed view that anyone who gets up at 5:30 in the morning to stand in line to tee off must be "out of his bird." So much for making friends. To keep us in the swim, or out of it, was going to take some careful balancing on my part—and a great wardrobe.

At that time, wearing whites on the tennis court was mandatory. I had no trouble buying and wearing an adorable little one-piece number for myself, but when I laid out the tennis whites I'd bought for my husband, he looked at me as if I'd had too much sun (never too strong a possibility in my case).

"How can I garden in these?" he asked, turning them over looking for the spots and stains he loved so well.

"You can't," I replied honestly, smoothing out my own snowy white skort. "We're going over to the courts to watch the kids play." (I had made sure our children would never find themselves in our socially unacceptable situation.)

"Why do I have to look like a damn dove to do that?" he bellowed.

"C'mon, dear, hurry," I answered. "We'll be late."

Happily, the outfits worked like a charm. A couple sitting next to us in the stands, who might have leaned across us to talk to a sportsman on our left or right B.O. (Before Outfits), now confided in us how good or bad the server was or where a particular shot would fall. It was *our* shoulders that were being nudged. "Hey, did you see that return?" Or "How 'bout that boy?"

Once I got into the swing of tennis, I had the confidence to move on to skiing. This sport actually left me cold, but I *did* love the atmosphere. I could sit in front of the huge, open fireplace, in the chalet-type ski lodge I loved, put my after-ski boots on an ottoman, dip my pecans in fondue, and engage in lively conversation. Well, *I* was lively. Sometimes the person I was talking to dozed off in the middle of a sentence. I didn't take this personally, because, unlike me, he or she might actually have spent eight hours on the slopes.

During the day, while the children (having a better childhood than *I* ever had) were off to the mountain, I was just another skier (wink, wink) dressed like all the other skiers, sipping hot chocolate to keep warm and dunking doughnuts for energy. To look at me in my stunning down jacket, slim pants, and jaunty cap, anybody might have thought I was fresh off the advanced slope after a two-hour run, rather than just recovering from a chill I'd gotten waiting to put the children on the chairlift.

The challenges were many, and I came through with flying colors (ones most flattering to me). One day in particular stands out vividly in my mind. I was with a crowd of people all waiting impatiently for his or her turn to water-ski. I had on one of my best-looking bathing suits, with my hair tied back to keep it from being whipped around by the wind. Naturally, I had no intention of letting it whip, but I looked ready for action. We drew lots. I was Number Three. Had I been less experienced in draft dodging, I might have recoiled in horror and shouted, "Water-ski? Me? You've got to be kidding," in which case I would have been sent back to the kiddie pool in disgrace. Instead, I volunteered to be the "watcher," on the ski boat. You're supposed to have two people on the ski boat, a driver and a "watcher," and here I was, an avid ski fan, making the supreme sacrifice—I was giving up my own turn to "watch" the others ski. How big could you get? They practically carried me to the boat on their shoulders.

As I told my friends later, the only thing that bothered me was I didn't get a chance to practice my water salute. Well, maybe next time. But not if I could help it. Dressing for the sport was as active as I cared to get, though there came the day when my dodge-'em car was about to be hit head-on. I was forced to use my last remaining ploy: the sports injury. Being slightly superstitious, I hesitated to take on the health fairy, but I was desperate. Some friends, thinking (I can't imagine why) that Babe Didrikson had been my mentor, signed me up for the local Women's Competition in Golf. When I saw my name on the list, I nearly fainted. It was going to take more than fancy golf shoes to get me out of this. What can I say? I'm not proud of what I did, but I did what I had to do.

Looking at the beaming faces around me, I took several sad breaths and said, "Gosh, would I love to do that, and maybe the doctor will let me, if I can just get rid of this darned tennis elbow in time."

You guessed it. My elbow never really healed. So now when someone asks if I play golf or tennis, or if I ski, I can sigh wistfully, point to my arm, and say with the air of someone who knows what it means to give up something she loves, "Not anymore."

With a *K*, and an *I*, and a *C*, *K*, *A*—

I was looking through some old letters the other day and found some correspondence between the owners of the summer camp my children attended and me. The names of the children have been changed for my protection.

January 5

Dear Mrs. Ward,

Coco and I are so very happy you have decided to let Jeffrey join us again at Camp Kickapee. We are planning a banner season at The Kick this year, and you will be glad to know we have greatly expanded our new facilities. For the first time, we will be offering horseback riding, archery, golf, and skeet shooting. In order for Jeffrey to be able to take full advantage of all sports, please note the following additions to our official camp list (see page 4 enclosed): riding pants, riding boots, helmet-type hat, riding crop, archer's mitt, golf clubs in lightweight bag, golf shoes, bow and arrow. If this necessitates using more than one regulation camp trunk, please be sure each piece is clearly marked in at least two places. We also ask that campers do not carry more than one small handbag on the bus.

You will be hearing from us, as camp time grows near, concerning Visiting Day, departure times, and camp regulations.

Once again, thank you for sending Jeffrey back to us.

Cordially,
Coco and Studs Hogarth

Dear Studs,

Jeffrey asked me to write you concerning the boys who will be sharing his tent this summer. It's always a little awkward to point the finger, but I think Jeff would be very unhappy if he found Killer Hanes in his bunk again this summer. It seems Tent Nine was never chosen as the Honor Tent, because the Hanes boy could not be persuaded to keep his hamsters and snakes in their cages. Every time the inspecting counselor stepped on a hamster, it was an automatic demerit. The lack of tent spirit was appalling. Therefore, we would appreciate it if you could relocate Killer. However, Jeff would still like to be in with Red Oppenheim, Bats Siegel, and Dutch Barnum if possible.

Thanks for your help.

Sincerely,
Lyla Ward

May 1

Dear Parents:

Impossible as it may seem, camp time is fast approaching. In this letter, you will find the time and place for departure and a few simple rules we feel are necessary for the well-being of our campers. By reading and observing the camp regulations, you will be ensuring the success of your own son's camping experience.

Departure: Bus departs White Horse Bus Terminal at 7 A.M. July 1. Please have your son at the terminal one half hour before departure time. Though the trip is only nine hours, we like to arrive at camp in time for the boys to jump right into the lake. Please do not bring dogs to the bus depot, as many children become emotional at the thought of leaving their pets. It is permissible, however, to bring younger or older siblings.

Rules: (Please keep these rules in a convenient location)

• No candy, cookies, soda, or gum will be accepted for campers. Do not include any of these in your packages. All sweets will be confiscated on discovery. To our disappointment, in other years, we have found candy hidden in pajama pockets, sneakers, boxes of stationery, etc. We urge you to cooperate.

• Special medication and prescriptions will be kept in the infirmary. Please be sure each bottle is clearly marked with the camper's name and dosage. Be sure eyeglasses, braces, and retainers are similarly marked.

Visiting Day: Parents will be welcome at camp on Saturday, July 28, at 10 A.M. Please do not bring bunk presents or gifts for counselors. Remember, camp is a present from you to your child, and he will not expect any other reward for attendance. Visiting Day will end at 4 P.M. on Saturday. At the whistle, please leave promptly. Prolonged leave-takings are difficult even for the happiest of campers.

Telephones: Please do not call camp unless an emergency arises. Your sons are required to write home three times a week, and we find homesickness is apt to follow calls from home.

We hope you will cooperate fully, and we look forward to a great Kickapee summer.

Cordially,
Coco and Studs Hogarth

July 9

Dear Mom and Dad,

How are you? I am fine. Camp is awful this year. You know what they went and did? They put Killer Hanes in a different tent. Now Tent Fourteen has all those neat hamsters and snakes. Bats Siegel turned real mean this year. I wish he would go home. Dutch Barnum's mother put Hershey bars inside his catcher's mitt, and they melted all over. It's so gooey inside his hand keeps slipping out. I hope you and Dad aren't going anywhere; I may want to come home.

Please send gum. You can put it in the comic books, they never look there. I have to go now. I'll finish this later.

Later.
Your loving son,
Jeff

If the Shoe Fits, Plant It

Not to boast, but I was doing flower arrangements when Martha Stewart was still in short pants. When I was a young hostess, the trend was toward Japanese-style arrangements: a single stalk on a shallow plate. Personally, I always went for a more abundant display: dramatic flashes of color, wildly creative containers, imaginative combinations of growing things—mangoes with turnips; clethras with asphodels; oxalises with celery and olives. Movement, flow, excitement. Even then I knew, if the centerpiece is compelling enough, you can forget about the food, which my guests did. Who was going to fuss about a few bones in the boneless chicken breasts if the wheat seems to be growing out of the persimmons in an antique stewpot?

Originality was and is the key. I never encouraged people to imitate my creations. I wanted everybody to have the abandon I had when it came to the use of flowers. There was the time I took my husband's favorite beer mug, filled it with beer, and floated a few roses in it, thus bringing our two passions together. Or the year my husband sent me a dozen roses for our anniversary. I didn't stick them in a tall vase with water and aspirin. They weren't sick. Instead, I took the whole dozen, cut off the stems, and strewed them around the house. When my husband came home, he was walking on the petals of his love. You can imagine how excited he was.

What I tried to convey, and what I say to young homemakers now, is, let loose, let your hair down, be free. And speaking of letting your hair down, after you've cut off the stems, instead of strewing, you may want to wind the roses into a coronet for your hair. What husband (or roommate) can resist his own little rose queen? Incidentally, don't throw away the stems. Dried rose stems can be substituted for wheat or corn husks if you need something for your clethras.

One thing Martha and I agree on is the importance of the container. We both think vases are so over. If you have one you're attached to, use it for storing pennies or curtain hooks, not flowers. Ms. Stewart very often uses small glasses of varying heights stuffed with oversize blooms. I say throw caution to the wind. Take a walk through all the rooms in your house in that free hour or two you have before your guests arrive. Look at everything with new eyes. Picture the candy dish: caramels out, anemones in. Or the sugar bowl: Splenda out, cactus in. Switch things around. Use the wastepaper basket for gladioli and snapdragons, the Baccarat vase for wastepaper. Skip into the kitchen. Here you'll find a gold mine of lovely holders: cups and saucers, blender jars, casseroles, ladles, electric skillets, saltshakers ad infinitum. If you don't have to worry about your container holding water, that is if you're using dried objects or fruit, you can really let your imagination run rampant. Use colanders, sewing baskets, jewelry boxes, canisters, food mills. Don't be afraid. Borrow from the children. You didn't say they could keep their crayons in that cookie jar forever. The important thing is daring and originality. If your container looks as if it were meant to hold flowers, you know you have the wrong dish.

By the same token, if you are using only flowers tucked neatly into a flower arranger, you're on the wrong track. Anyone can have an obviously beautiful centerpiece. What talent does that take? What you want is a showstopper like the arrangement I created for one of the best dinner parties I ever hosted. I happened to have some really lovely zinnias in bloom in my garden and some mildew-resistant asters. I could have simply stuck them into a square of arranging clay and covered that over with some pebbles. But I didn't. Do you know what I did? I reversed the whole thing. I took the zinnias and the asters, cut them into small pieces, and lined the bottom of a leopard-print lingerie box. Then I took the arranging clay and made the head of a sphinx (you *could* make anything; I happen to be good at sphinxes), and around this I put not only little colored pebbles but lots of rocks from outside, and set them down artistically on the cut-up asters. An obvious feeling of strength pervaded the arrangement, and when someone put a carrot stick in the sphinx's mouth, a wave of laughter spread around the table. I don't know when I've been on the receiving end of so much merriment. Everybody kept saying fun things like "The dinner sphinx" or "This is what I call a rock-and-rolls affair." It was absolutely hilarious. That dinner was a hard one to top.

Most of the time, you will find something around the house to use in an effective arrangement. But for those days when fresh items are in short supply, every serious arranger should have a ready stock of dried things. A lot of these are available in stores, but it is much less expensive if you dry your own. For this purpose, reserve a sunny spot in your house, preferably where you don't mind things hanging down from the ceiling. Entranceways and stall showers are out for obvious reasons. Now take a string and string it, clothesline fashion, from wall to wall. On this you can place your old rose stems, used corsages, corn husks, packets of pumpkin seeds, etc. A word of caution: I don't recommend drying your own fruit. Though prunes, pre-dried, are admittedly costly, I had plums strung up on my lines for two weeks, and the insides, instead of condensing properly as they seem to for the California people, simply dropped out, and there I was, left with a whole line of puckered skins.

Occasionally, you may be called on to improvise. You or your spouse may have impulsively invited some coworkers home for dinner. The flowers you hung up yesterday are not yet dry. Last week's rose petals are in the vacuum cleaner. What to do for a centerpiece? It might be the first thing you can lay your hands on; in my case, a 16th-century Ming Dynasty tea caddy. At such short notice you are admittedly stuck for greenery. But don't overlook the common plants to be found in every household. What could be more fragile than dainty celery leaves or greener than fresh watercress? (You can put potatoes around the meat.) If you don't have enough fruit to be lavish, cut each piece in half and place it pit side down, or use thinly sliced oranges to simulate the rays of the sun. There are all sorts of ways to improvise. The important thing is to use what you have and make it work.

Once you've found a rare container and selected materials others might have put down the Disposall, you must now put them together in a free, uninhibited manner. For best effect, forget about balance. Nothing is duller than an even arrangement. It's true, some guests are a bit hurt when they are seated at the backside of an arrangement, but artistry cannot be compromised. Suppose you were to take a beautiful, large eggplant and set it to one side of your Lowestoft meat platter. Does that mean you have to take another large eggplant and put it at the other side? Certainly not. Take a zucchini or a bunch of radishes (out of the plastic wrapper) or some green beans, and put *them* at the other end. If possible, have a square of Styrofoam soaking at all times; then at the last minute, you can stick in anything available from your drying line: old chrysanthemums, gladioli, petrified baby's breath. A stalk here, a stalk there, placed completely at random, and you will have *some* centerpiece.

I think I have proved flower arranging is simple. The key, and this cannot be stressed enough, is originality. If you prefer a centerpiece that cannot be eaten, dried flowers or uncooked vegetables are for you. If you don't mind being left with the skeleton of a bunch of grapes, a living centerpiece may be your answer. But whatever you choose, make it your own creation; something that will cause the guest entering your dining room to stop, stare, and exclaim, "My God, look what she's got in the center of the table!" That, my friends, is the sound of success.

ON THE PRESENT (TENSE)

If life gets confusing,
Don't worry: that's when you
Can press Option One
And return to Main Menu.

Private Lives

I have now been assured by four banks, my mutual fund, Talbots, two insurance companies, Visa, American Express, Bloomingdale's, my mortgage company, the electric company, and Macy's that I need have no fears about my privacy.

As required by federal law, each of these institutions and others have sent me a pamphlet describing in detail how they've gathered what they call "nonpublic information" about me. It seems under this strict regulation, they're allowed to call just about anybody who knows or has ever known me, in a financial sense. The department store can call the bank to find out if I really have an account there. The mortgage company can call my employer to find out if I'm really employed there. The credit bureau stands ready and willing to fill in the dots for any subscriber who wants to know what the bank, the department store, or the mortgage company really thinks of me.

But not to worry. On the next page of the notice, I am reassured that my personal information is "in the vault" because my government has taken these important steps to protect my privacy. Even though they know more about me than my mother, they're sworn to secrecy. The law is clear. They can only share this information with the company's immediate "corporate family," of which there are perhaps 500 or 1,000 affiliates, as well as any companies that provide services to the parent company and a few outsiders, such as banks, loan brokers, account aggregators, insurance agents, insurance companies, mortgage banks, securities brokers, retailers, direct marketers, communication companies, Internet service providers, manufacturers, service companies, travel agents, cruise lines, car rental agencies, hotels, airlines, publishers, and nonprofit organizations.

In fact, the only one who can't get information about me without providing my Social Security number, or tax ID, or my mother's maiden name, under this most stringent of laws, is me.

But again, not to worry. While I can't turn off the information spout to any of the companies for whom I have filled out an application somewhere at some point in time (and if I don't want this stuff broadcast over the airwaves), there are steps I can take to stop it. All I have to do is write each one of them and their affiliates and their marketing consultants, etc., and tell them not to give out my personal information to anyone not specifically allowed by law. This shouldn't amount to more than a thousand letters, which I can easily do in my spare years.

Aside from the carload of printed official Privacy Notifications, every time I go shopping online, a Privacy Policy box appears on the screen, and guess what? All the e-companies with whom I've shared my charge account numbers, my e-mail address, and, in some cases, my whole shopping history (because otherwise they wouldn't even let me "walk" into their "showroom") are going to protect my private information with the same vigor as all the banks, the stores, and their corporate families.

So I'm legally covered. My government has seen to that. Why then, do I have this lingering feeling I'm so completely exposed? Notified, shmotified, my life is an open book for which I get no royalties. And what's more, anybody can read it, everybody can sell it, and nobody has to pay *me* for any of it.

And Miles to Go Before I Reap

Do you know what I like best about frequent-flier miles? You don't have to fly to get them. In fact, I do better by buying than flying.

Why should I fly 3,000 miles and spend five or six hours on a plane to get a measly 1,000 frequent-flier miles, when I can earn 10,000 FFMs just by changing my long-distance telephone carrier? Hey, if I can still dial out and the miles are right, I don't care who's holding the wires.

The offers are everywhere. They're tucked inside my Visa bill; they're advertised in the newspapers; they come in the mail: 5,000 miles for shopping at *this* store, 3,000 miles for filling up at *that* station. Recently, I had my choice of staying at a Marriott in Cincinnati or a Hilton in Cleveland. The Marriott was offering 5,000 bonus miles for an overnight stay, and the Hilton was offering nada. It was a no-brainer. Naturally, I stayed in Cincinnati, which isn't all that far from Cleveland, where my daughter lives.

Flexibility, that's the key. It's like couponing. You can't get hung up on brands or manufacturers. You have to go where the miles are. That's why I'm no longer driving a Honda. I really liked my little car. And I would still be driving it today if the dealer had been willing to meet me halfway, maybe even thrown in a few thousand FFMs. But when a 15,000-mile offer came along just for driving this Big Mama out of the showroom, how could I refuse? *Fifteen thousand miles*, and all I had to do was give up the car I loved. Plus, there was the hidden value: I get extra mileage at the gas pump for filling up every day.

While I admit I prefer the Big Offers, I take what I can. Mileage for renting certain cars, using certain products, shopping on certain Web sites, subscribing to certain publications, eating at uncertain restaurants. I do it all. No wonder I have more mileage in the bank than dollars, which means, even if I have trouble paying the rent in my later years, I'll be able to accept a dinner invitation anywhere in the world.

There are those who think the airlines should abandon their frequent-flier programs, concentrate on lowering their rates, and compete with one another on the basis of price and service—I disagree. At least for now. I almost have the 200,000 miles I need for my trip to Outer Mongolia. And as soon as I have mine, I'm going to start on my husband's, so *this* time, we can go together.

Pressed for Time

Whoever thought of telephone menus is a genius. Every office has one. These days, even when I want to talk to my doctor, I have to know what to press.

Not that I'm complaining. Au contraire. It's such fun listening to all my options, I've decided to create a menu of my own. From now on, whenever you or anyone you know calls me, this is what you'll hear:

"Thank you for calling the home of Lyla and Russell Ward. If you are calling from a touch-tone phone, press 1. If not, press 2. If you know your party's extension, you can dial it at any time. If you are calling for Lyla, press 1. If you are calling for Russell, press 2. (We have two lines. If one screeches, you've accidentally dialed the fax.)"

Music will swell in the background. It's the ever popular "V'ho ingannato," the death scene duet from Rigoletto, *which doesn't run more than five or six minutes. Then, in a friendly, personal tone, I'll thank you for your patience and ask that you listen carefully to the following options:*

"If you are a deliveryman who is three hours late in delivering the refrigerator and has gotten lost, press 1. If you are the owner of the parked car I left a note on, press 2. If you are calling to ask why I missed the dentist appointment you forced me to make six months ago when I was in your office and didn't have a chance to look at my very full calendar at home, press 3. If you are a family member and would like to speak to your mother, press 4. If you are calling to reschedule the dentist appointment, press 5. If you are offering an unbeatable price on refinancing our house, selling our house, cleaning our chimneys, consolidating our debt, changing our long-distance carrier, spraying for ticks, dial 0 for operator. (We don't have one.)"

You are the deliveryman, and you pressed 1: "If you want to reach our house coming north on the thruway, press 1. If you want to reach our house coming south on the thruway, press 2. If you want to reach our house coming east on the parkway, press 3. If you want to reach our house coming west on the parkway, press 4. For all other directions, press 5."

You are the owner of the badly parked car, and you pressed 2: "At the tone, please leave your name, address, telephone number, the name and number of your insurance company, your motor vehicle registration, Social Security number, the number of your driver's license, and the time and date of your birth."

You are calling about a missed dentist appointment, and you pressed 3: "The dog ate my appointment book."

You are my daughter, and you pressed 4: "Hi, honey, this is your mother. I meant to tell you I changed your button to 4. But if you've forgotten where we live, follow the directions for the deliveryman. At the tone, leave a message."

You are calling about rescheduling a dentist appointment, and you pressed 5: "I'll buzz you as soon as my phone is fixed."

Granted, this is only a rough draft, but you get the idea. I just want *my* callers to enjoy the same options they extend to me. My menu is as simple and efficient as any I've encountered. And I'm sure everyone will be as happy as I am to spend 10 extra minutes per call as long as it is so rewarding to stay on the line.

Border Lines

When I'm not trying to think of a graceful way out of Iraq, or how to get China to buy more of our (still made in this country) low-fat cream cheese, I ponder the problem of illegal immigration. With all due respect to those worthy legislators who have pushed for the 700-mile fence along the 2,000-mile border, or guest-worker programs, or out-and-out amnesty, what are the real chances of any of these steps doing the trick? My pondering has led me to believe: zilch, zero, *ninguno*. So why don't we just end the rhetoric, put Lou Dobbs out of his misery, pool the fence and increased Border Patrol uniform money, and (111th Congress, take note) *buy* Mexico?

I know, I know. It's not on Craigslist, but everything has its price, and we have some world-class mergers-and-acquisitionists in this country. Plus, it's been a long time since we bought a neighbor, 207 years to be exact. And though there have been rumors that, after Katrina, some in this administration tried to get France to take her back, on the whole, Louisiana has proved to be a pretty good investment.

As to the price, it wouldn't be as expensive as you

might think. We bought Louisiana (51,843 square miles) for about $940,000 in 1803. That works out to about $18 and change, per square mile. Mexico is 761,606 square miles, and the value of the dollar today is about 45 times what it was in 1803. That means we should be able to pick her up for about $616 million.

Cheap, when you consider it's costing us about $177 million a day to continue the war in Iraq, which we won't even own when we're through. Add to that the obvious advantage to both the U.S. and the people of Mexico if this deal were to go through, and Mexico were to become the 51st state.

Most of the 12 to 20 million undocumented workers would probably want to head home right away. This would mean a good piece of change for Greyhound, because with only 52 seats on each bus, this illegal movement would involve anywhere from 230,769 to 384,615 trips.

Once back in the now State of Mexico, those workers who made less than minimum wage with no benefits in the U.S. would be assured of $7.25 an hour—if they found jobs. "If," because at this point Mexico would no longer be considered a cheap labor market, and its jobs would have been exported to China or Qatar, and its workers would have to suck it up like other Americans.

Still, once legal, they would be entitled to unemployment insurance or even welfare until they could be retrained for the corporate job market, which would undoubtedly begin to surge as corporations, without seeming unpatriotic, could move their headquarters to a politically correct paradise. Given the choice, it's hard to picture a CEO picking Princeton, NJ, over Guadalajara.

Even if we were to throw in a few mink pelts and some amber fields of grain to sweeten the pot (no offense meant), we would still be ahead of the game. Illegal aliens cost the government upwards of $61 billion a year and an estimated $311 billion in uncollected taxes. Once Mexico was a state of the union, some say their own oil and gas revenues could pay for the acquisition alone.

No doubt President Calderón—who is apparently as anxious to export Mexicans as they are to leave—might raise some objections, because as a senator (assuming he was elected), he would not have as much influence over U.S. foreign policy as he does now, being Mexican president. But he's a smart guy, and once he saw the health benefits package and the travel opportunities, he'd probably jump at the chance to be an official part of the U.S. government.

What it boils down to is this: if everyone in the country—we're a nation of 300 million—shelled out $2.05 each, we could buy Mexico without raising taxes. We wouldn't have to bring our National Guard troops back from Iraq to guard the borders; drug smuggling would become an obsolete term as we would just "trade" brother to brother; and with more people able to retire to Acapulco without losing their Medicare benefits, Florida would be less likely to sink from overpopulation.

The choice is ours. We can continue to have our lowest-paying jobs filled by foreigners, or we can reserve them for our own people—our newest citizens. Write your congressman today. Viva Mexico, USA.

The Business of Business

I have always been as opposed to Big Business as my Republican friends are to Big Government. But as more and more buildings, theaters, athletic stadiums begin to bear the name of their corporate sponsors, I'm beginning to reconsider. If "American Airlines" is now emblazoned across a theater in New York and the show still goes on (*and* you may get frequent-flier miles to attend), what harm? The idea of allowing our generous corporate citizens to share the expense of our public buildings and national monuments, as well as skyscrapers and auditoriums, is beginning to sound pretty good. So we put their names up in neon lights, is that so bad? Would it make the Library of Congress any less of an institution if it were called the Barnes and Noble Library of Congress? The same records would still be there, and the library could perk up its site by adding a list of best sellers to its home page.

The more I think about it, the more possibilities I see for a profitable partnership between business and government. Just by allowing the most subtle advertising, we taxpayers could save a bundle. Picture this:

The Sherwin-Williams White House: We paint every four years. There's no repeel.
General Motors Interstate 95: Better roads for better cars.
Scotchgard's Smithsonian Institute: Preservation is our only business.
Smith Barney's Social Security: You earned it!
Energizer's U.S. Senate: Keeps going and going and going.
ILGWU's Lincoln Memorial: Look for the Union label.
Jockey Underwear's House of Representatives: The best seat in the House.
Rolaid's Mount Rushmore: How do you spell *relief*?
Maxwell House Coffee's Grand Canyon: Good to the last drop.
General Electric's Department of Energy: We bring good things to life.
Volkswagen's Pentagon: Think small.
Taco Bell's Department of Immigration: Head for the border.
Coca-Cola's Supreme Court: The laws that refresh.
General Foods' Jefferson Memorial: Celebrate the monuments of your life.

Not too shabby, and the best part is: at last Republicans and Democrats can each claim victory for their principles. Taxpayer dollars will no longer be paying for government excesses. The private sector will. And if that's not finger lickin' good, you've never tasted Kentucky Fried Chicken.

TV U

I was once at a dinner party where most of the guests were lawyers. I am not. But if I do say so myself, when it came to how many "exculpatories" or "inadmissibles" could be used in one sentence, no one at the table could hold a candle to me, though I had the feeling some would have liked to.

As an avid student of the legal process, from *Perry Mason* to *Law & Order,* I have probably spent more time in court than most trial attorneys. That's how I know when someone says, "Voir dire," he's not making a pass at me. So don't tell *me* television is not educational!

Knowledgeable as I am about the law, it's not my only paraprofession. I have learned enough about medicine from *Dr. Kildare* to *ER* to easily diagnose a myocardial infarction, should one unhappily present itself. Or if someone was missing a heartbeat, I don't think I'd have a problem thumping his chest with or without a resuscitator. There's not an illness known to man whose symptoms I don't now know and dream of every Tuesday and Thursday, thanks to these wonderful tutorials.

And let's not forget forensics. I can't, because so many of

my hours have been spent at the morgue, from *Dr. Quincy* to *Crossing Jordan* to *CSI*. And though I might not be able to officiate at a cadaver event, these MEs have kept me on the cutting edge of forensics for more than 20 years.

It was Quincy who was my first forensics teacher. In that early show, the closest we came to viewing an actual autopsy was in the opening scene, where Quincy is starting to demonstrate his carving technique for the new students, and one by one, like so many dominoes, they faint and fall to the ground. Wimps. As the shows have grown more graphic over the years, I have sat, unflinching, popcorn on my lap, while an enthusiastic medical examiner cracks open a cranial cavity to reveal the telltale damage to the left frontal lobe. And I'm proud to say, as soon as the ME shows me the bruises and the congealed blood surrounding them, I can tell if the attacker was right- or left-handed, wore a size 10 or 11 shoe (D or E width), weighed between 180 and 182 pounds, was male or female or a cross-dresser, and whether or not the perp had French toast for breakfast (which is clearly indicated by the egg-soaked crumbs on the victim's forehead). I am also fairly adept at reading X-rays. I can tell by looking at that little squiggly line next to the small shadow near the ventricular cortex that 10 years ago in September, the victim sustained a similar blow unrelated to the one that blew her out of the box at 10:55 on that fateful evening.

Is it any wonder I spring to the defense of television when I hear it so widely criticized and rarely credited for the wealth of information it has given us over the years? I shudder to think of those days before I knew what spousal privilege meant or what could happen if one were to ignore symptoms of PMS or MSP, or any one of a dozen syndromes. For me, the legal process, medicine, forensics are just the beginning. I'm looking forward to the fall lineup when, rumor has it, there will be an exciting new show: *Jaw and Order,* an in-depth look at dental work for the criminally insane. I've got my fingers crossed it's not just word of mouth.

Some Don't Like It Hot

Enough about how many Mexicans have entered this country illegally and are taking the low-paying jobs that Americans looking for low-paying jobs might otherwise be taking. Sure, this is a serious problem that probably should have been addressed before the *last* election, but for some of us, that's not the whole enchilada.

What gets my blood boiling are all those peppery plants that have been crossing the border, unchallenged, for years. Chipotles, habaneros, manzanos, poblanos. Is mine the only palate that rebels against the inclusion of jalapeños on my plate of ham and eggs? How sad is that when even our local diner unabashedly features breakfast burritos, and with apologies to no one, puts salsa, now the number-one-selling national condiment, on the table next to that defeated champion, ketchup. Is it any wonder we heat wimps are feeling the chili winds of change?

The sad truth is, over the past 10 or 15 years, a tidal wave of spicy food has washed over the kitchens of our formerly bland republic. Chefs all around town, in every town, choose cilantro, a dead ringer for parsley, as the national herb. So when you start eating the greenery temptingly arranged around the sirloin steak, you never know if your tongue is going to be pleasantly titillated by those mild green leaves you once knew and loved, or if the inside of your mouth is going to be assaulted by the hot reality of a plant fire.

Nor does one have to go to an exotic Mexican market to buy herbs like cilantro. The produce section of every supermarket in America places it side by side with its look-alike, Italian parsley, not far from those darling little green tomatoes you expect to change into the rosy vegetable/fruit you might use for a Tuna Surprise. Don't hold your breath. Chances are, these immature love apples are really tomatillos, a Mexican variety that, as it ripens, turns yellow and is so tart it's been known to bring tears to the eyes of even the bravest of caballeros.

If these invaders of our territory had been content to confine their ethnic offerings to restaurants clearly identifiable by their names—El Tostado, Burritos R'Us, Cumin Inn, as other immigrant groups have before them (e.g., Reno Cappuccino)—we could have passed them by, secure in our knowledge that at *our* restaurant we could still feel safe biting into a slice of apple pie. As things stand now, you never know when a hot tamale may find its way into an otherwise perfect blend of natural grain granola.

Which is not to say I am totally opposed to all things Latin. I've been known to swizzle a margarita, with or without salt on the rim, with the best of them. The problem here is one of dilution. Alls I'm saying is, when I go to my neighborhood restaurant and order a side of French fries, a truly American dish, I want to be darn sure it doesn't have any foreign influences.

Lady in Waiting

News item: AT&T Wireless has begun charging for calls that go unanswered for more than 30 seconds, or approximately six rings. The caller will be charged for all rings after that.

What a great idea: charging for waiting time. I've been looking for a way to increase my income, plump up my bottom line, so to speak, and I think this may be it.

Businesses everywhere have been adding service charges like crazy. Some hotels are charging a "connectivity fee" for access to the phone, Internet, or fax, whether or not you actually use the service. Theatergoers, who stand on line in the cold at the box office, are being charged the same service charge they would pay if they were snug at home and had ordered tickets online or by phone. And the list goes on. Hard times call for hard choices. I don't have anything anyone would want to see, so I can't sell tickets. And I think it would be chintzy to charge my guests for using my phone, so I've decided to take a page out of the telephone company's book. From now on, any company with whom I do business will find out: my time is their time, but for a price.

Verizon: take note. Last week I had trouble with my home phone. When I called the repair service, I was held on the line for 14 thank-you-for-your-patience minutes. During this time, in which I was treated to a recitation of the company's services around the world, I could not respond to any incoming calls or receive a fax (we're deprived, we have only one line). And because you can't really rest a portable on your shoulder, I did not have the use of my hands, which otherwise would have been whipping up a soufflé or tying sailors' knots. Under my new wait-compensation system, I've decided to charge the telephone company what they charge me. At the telephone repairman's rate of $65 for the first half hour, the telephone company will owe me $30.33, which I plan to deduct from my bill. And if they threaten to cut off my service, I just may retaliate by getting another company (from Alaska, maybe) to do my repairs.

Which brings me to the $23.90 a month my Internet provider charges to my American Express account. As a recreational user, I don't want to spring for broadband or DSL, so I'm stuck with the familiar delaying messages: "Do you want to continue running script on this page?" Or "The modem has failed to connect . . . Attempt Number One . . . Attempt Number Two . . . Attempt Number Three," and on and on. When I am finally connected, after five or six minutes, I don't even have time to read my spam. My fantasy would be to charge the company for my pain and suffering, but the reality is I'll just have to ask for *their* American Express number and charge a nominal fee, say two months' free service.

Don't tell me. I'm way ahead of you. I know I'm not going to get rich charging for my time, particularly at these low rates, but a little here, a little there helps pay for the Prozac. And who knows? If I can work out a way to charge my doctor for the time between my two o'clock appointment and three o'clock when he finally takes me, or the delivery man who tells me if I call at 7 A.M., the day of the scheduled delivery, he will pin down my couch's arrival to morning or afternoon, or the plumber who will be at my house between 10 A.M. and 4 P.M., *then* we'll be talking big bucks.

Whether AT&T, my role model, and I can pull this off remains to be seen, but I'm cool. I've taken the important first steps. Now I'll just have to wait and fee.

Life in a Bubble

Here's the thing. We just had our house appraised and, *gulp*, it's worth five times what we paid for it 12 years ago. If we do the math, which we did rather quickly, we're sitting on a fortune; playing with a full deck *and* patio. Who would ever have thought our little weathered cottage, a half block from a private ocean beach, would cause us to rewrite our wills and totally rethink our lifestyle? Because let's face it, you just don't treat a million-plus house the way you would a bungalow in the low hundred thousands.

For openers, what *was* our little home by the sea is now a Property, and as such deserves to be maintained in a manner befitting its market price. Translation: our days as do-it-yourselfers are over. We wouldn't even know where to buy the kind of nails you put into a house of this value. Painting, caulking, filling in the little cracks with wood putty—uh-uh. Not for people of our new net worth. True, professionals who do jobs like this may charge $30 or $40 an hour. But how insignificant is that when you're talking a million-plus Property?

Another thing we've learned is that treating our Property properly also means getting rid of our penny-pinching ways when it comes to home improvement. Before our rise in circumstance, if we needed a little extra screening in our backyard, now referred to only as "in back," we might have opted for white pines and forsythia. *Quel bourgeois* for a Property. Now we're more likely to gravitate toward the Japanese cedars and Arabian jasmine. A bit pricey, sure, but in our bracket cost is hardly an issue. And while we're at it, it's unlikely you'll be seeing those old $4-a-pot geraniums in our window boxes. Our vision now is to have the kind of plants that more closely reflect our newly elevated taste. Perhaps a few leatherleaf sedges rubbing shoulders with some Bellania Beas.

And it doesn't stop there. Our wardrobes, once limited to faded Levi's and Fort Myers Beach T-shirts, perfectly appropriate for owners of a modest house on less than half an acre, now make us look deliberately underdressed, as if to mock those whose houses are not in the million-dollar-plus class. We're shopping for designer jeans we fit into and maybe some of those Ralph Lauren tops we've seen on other millionaires.

Still, even when the clouds have silver linings or, in our case, gold, clouds remain, and this is what we're dealing with now. On the one hand, unless we sell our house, which we have no intention of doing, we have no more money than we had the week before we found out our house was considered a Property. But on the other hand, we can only afford to keep up our Property in the manner it deserves if we sell it. It's a conundrum. Not only that, it's a tricky problem that gnaws at us even as we're hiring someone to glaze the floors.

Don't think we're not grateful for this real-estate boom that has catapulted us into the upper brackets of society. We do recognize the value of our worth. It's just that every so often, when we hear the current market described as a "bubble," we're rooting for the side with the pins.

How to Live in the Hamptons Without Ever Seeing a Celebrity

I live in Amagansett, which is owned by East Hampton, much of the year. And I'm here to tell you I have never laid eyes on a celebrity. Not Alec Baldwin, not Kim Basinger. Not Martha Stewart, not Jerry Seinfeld. Not Kathleen Turner, not Paul Simon. Not Steven Spielberg, not Ralph Lauren. I've never seen Jerry Della Femina, would you believe?

I seem always to arrive two minutes after Someone has just been there. A little flutter of excitement will still be in the air as I walk into the Farmers' Market. "That was Christie Brinkley," I'll hear another customer whisper to her friend. But by the time I turn around, she's gone. Or "Did you see Lee Radziwill?" I swivel—just in time to see the hairdresser from a local beauty parlor. No princess. No celebrity.

Either I arrive just after Someone's been there or just before They come. I was on the exact spot on Main Street only 15 minutes before Hillary Clinton showed up. If I had waited to see her, my ice cream would have melted. A couple of years before, I missed Bill Clinton by a hair. I was annoyed because the crowd gathering around the fire station in Amagansett was holding up traffic, relieved when I got by it, and surprised later to discover they were waiting for the President.

It's not as if I don't know what these people look like. Every week, the local papers have pages of photos of famous people attending the many benefits that attract famous people. Their faces are etched in my mind, though I'm not sure I would recognize some of the women without their spaghetti straps. I suppose if I really wanted to see Someone, I would pay the $500, invest in some spandex capri pants, and share a plate with Edward Albee. My curiosity stops just short of a hundred dollars, and for that, you get only starlets whose upcoming TV series may or may not be picked up by the network.

One year, Macaulay Culkin's family rented a house right on the beach at the end of the street where I live. You might say we shared a beach. We saw everyone in the family except for Macaulay, who either didn't come or sunbathed at night, because I never laid eyes on him.

I feel so terribly out of it when I read Who spends the summer in the Hamptons. I wonder how I manage to miss Everybody. I shop in the Beautiful Stores, I eat in the Beautiful Restaurants, I walk on the gold-lined streets. How come Caroline Kennedy Schlossberg never crosses my path?

I don't doubt They're here. There isn't a real-estate agent in town who hasn't sold a house to Somebody. Still, as far as I'm concerned, They might all be vacationing on Lake Erie. They're like those invisible sand creatures one finds on the beach, No-See-Ums.

And My Vote Goes To …

Finally, this is my year! I am a white, older woman, ardent supporter of Hillary Clinton, now being wooed by Republicans and Democrats alike. How great is that! I cast my first vote for Adlai Stevenson in 1952, but this is the first time any political party ever singled me out for attention.

Sure, my pre-election mail has always been full of self-addressed envelopes that told me how much my support (code word: donation) would mean to this or that candidate, but I've been old and white and of course a woman for quite a few years now, and no one has ever made me feel special. All the speeches, the TV commercials, and interviews with party muckamucks have focused on the swing vote. Independents have always been the darlings of every campaign. I was just a part of the base, my vote taken for granted, my demographic not worthy of mention.

Now, happy day, all eyes are on my group: the over-65 female crowd. It would seem I, and others answering my description, hold the pivotal vote. The questions are flying. Am I so bitter about Hillary's defeat that I will vote for John McCain? Do I find the nomination of Sarah Palin offensive enough to make me vote for Obama? Maybe. And maybe. I haven't made my mind up yet, but I'm willing to listen to both sides, and not only do I have the time to do it (remember, I'm retired), I'm loving it.

I particularly enjoy hearing the male commentators, political strategists, and pundits speak authoritatively about why we (*my* group) will never vote for Obama. Too young, too inexperienced, and, worst of all, not a woman. After all, we came of age with Betty Friedan, Kate Millett, Gloria Steinem. We wouldn't stand for a man, even an African American, snatching the nomination away from *our* candidate.

Will we instead embrace Sarah Palin? Young, yes, but a woman. Against a woman's right to choose? Yes, but a woman. A self-described barracuda? Yes, but a woman. And since *my group,* according to *this group,* was leaning toward McCain anyway, if we couldn't have Hillary Clinton, we would vote for McCain. He knows, firsthand, what it's like to be old, and with him we can at least trade Medicare stories.

What a kick! I wish I could have been in Florida (we're there from January through March) to hear Senator Clinton's speech to my fellow seniors. It's a great place to campaign, what with the price of gas and all, because the golf communities are so close together a politician can hit a lot of old people in one day.

To get back to the question of who will get my vote. Unfortunately, I'm not in a position to offer the formerly-for-Hillary-older-woman vote to any candidate. My organizing days are over. Make no mistake, even if it rains on

November 4, I will vote, and my friends will vote, and we're leaning (literally) toward—? Tell me again, John, Barack (you won't mind if I call you by your first name since your letters always call me by mine), how important *am* I to you? Do you really think my vote will swing the election? Is *my* group really more important than the Independents?

Okay, okay, I guess I trust you. I just wish your noses would stop growing.

Driving Lessons

Though the new administration has not specifically asked for my help, I have nevertheless wracked my brain trying to come up with ways to solve the energy crisis. Because I live in a condo, drilling for oil in my backyard is out of the question. And the board won't even let me put a satellite dish on my roof, no less a windmill, so what to do?

While the politicians are busy exploring ways to increase fuel efficiency by the year 3000 (by which time we'll all, well, not *all,* be driving in our cars and gasping for breath), I have worked out a few ideas that are ready to go on Day One. These suggestions are free for the taking: no need to log on and subscribe to a green newsletter, or contribute to HOG (Hoard Our Gas). Just take your foot off the gas pedal and:

Coast. Wherever possible, drive downhill. At first look, this may seem impractical because of the well-known adage "What goes down must go up," but don't be fooled. There are still many low-level roads to be traveled.

Buy one *less* car. In many homes, each teenager has his or her own car, meaning many families have four or five cars. To save fuel, eliminate at least one. Mom and Dad won't mind sharing.

Join a car pool. It may take a while to find four other people who use the same dentist as you do, but think of the gas you'll save, and of all those back copies of *National Geographic* you'll get to read while you wait for the other four to have root canal or cap replacements.

Be inventive. If you have to commute by car, because there is no mass transit between East Gator and West Croc, where the factory is located, suggest to your boss that the company institute a work-at-home plan. Help him to see the savings involved in assembling airplane parts off-site.

Make friends with the gas station attendant. Bribe him to call you just before he posts the new gas prices. That way you can hurry down and fill up for 50 cents a gallon less than you would have to pay an hour later, when he changes the prices again.

Group your errands. If your dry-cleaning won't be ready until Wednesday, and your mother-in-law's plane is due on Tuesday, ask her to change her flight so that you can pick up your cleaning on the way home rather than make a special trip.

Go back to the city. The suburbs are gas guzzlers. In these clogged arteries of the metropolis, the hardware store is five miles from the supermarket that's eight miles from the gym that's ten miles in the other direction from home.

The burbs have had their day. Now it's over. Everyone back to the city, where Pepcid takes care of the gas situation.

If none of these ideas seem to grab you, and writing to your congressman means getting a rambling letter from the 15-year-old intern who has volunteered to answer his mail, you may want to consider going back to a horse and buggy. At least then you would know, the more you drive, the greener the grass.

On the Up and Up

Slowly, stealthily, I've been upgraded. Before Starbucks came on the scene, I had never paid more than a dollar for a cup of coffee in my life. Stepping up to the counter for the first time and shelling out $1.45 (now $1.75) for a tall (small) decaf didn't seem so much to pay when others around me were nonchalantly peeling off five-dollar bills (keep the change) for a latte or a frappuccino, concoctions only loosely related to the plain pre-Starbucks cup of coffee I used to pick up at the corner store on my way to work.

It took me a couple of boxes of Berry Burst Cheerios to know what was happening to my budget. Now, at last, I get it. Price index notwithstanding, I am spending more for new versions of my old products. I'm being upgraded on a daily basis. It almost seems déclassé to buy unadulterated Total without even a hint of dried fruit or granola or cinnamon added, and it only costs a little bit more.

Oreos have been a favorite of mine for years. Oreos, those little chocolate cookies with the sugary white filling inside. Try finding a package of old-fashioned Oreos. Not a chance. For an additional 30 or 40 cents you can have double-stuffed, chocolate-filled, or candy-coated. Plain Oreos? They just ran out.

Frozen green beans were always good to go, until frozen green beans with mushrooms, or frozen green beans with onions or water chestnuts, found their way into the freezer case. Now the original plain ones look, well, plain, next to the combos, and they only cost a few cents—okay, maybe 50 cents—more.

All the old plain products I used to buy now contain nuts, M&M's, raisins, Reese's Pieces, Toll House bits. Specialty items formerly carried only in gourmet stores now line the shelves of the most ordinary supermarket. Tea, for instance. Plain old Lipton's tea was fine for me, until one day fancier teas began to appear on the supermarket shelf. How could I resist? The few extra cents a drink was cheaper than a trip to England, so I tried Twinings. It was three times the price of Lipton, but, hey, I only drink one or two cups a day. No point in denying myself for a few measly cents a day.

Soon, a whole variety of other mixtures joined their English cousins. Green tea (twice the price of Lipton) is touted to be extra good for you; it provides antioxidants (whatever they are). I also found chamomile to relax me and ginger to soothe my stomach; each one carrying a price tag two or three times more than the plain old I used to drink each afternoon before I met the others.

The amazing part of all this is shelf space. Market size notwithstanding, there is a finite amount of room available to display an ever-growing number of products. In the produce department, we have the original carrots and the organic carrots, the original zucchini and the organic zucchini. Each fruit or vegetable grown with frowned-upon fertilizers has a counterpart nurtured with eco-friendly, humane soil enhancers. Guilt is reaching for the less expensive peach that may have, however innocently, contributed to greenhouse gas emissions.

Once I realized what was happening, I tried to find and buy my old choice, in most cases now labeled "Original." Each time I shop, the Original gets harder to find. Fresh orange juice, not from concentrate, used to be just fresh orange juice not from concentrate, either a quart or a half gallon. Now Tropicana or Florida's Natural has juice with no pulp, a little pulp, or a lot of pulp, with added calcium or without added calcium. The orange juice section of the refrigerator case is outspacing the yogurts, which run from the Original plain to strawberry, blueberry, apple, peach, boysenberry, and vanilla, with either a sugar substitute added (or not) or granola added (or not), from five different brands.

Where this will all end (graham crackers with papaya filling for an extra 60 cents?), I'm not sure. But I can see the day coming when we will have to pay more for the Originals because they're in such short supply. And looking to the future, I have a vision of these empty cartons on display in the Smithsonian for some child in 2108 to look at and say to a doubting friend, "See, I *told* you they used to have orange juice without jelly beans in it."

Wait and Switch

Here's the story. Elections are all about red and blue states—and undecided voters. Over and over again we were told, registered Democrats and Republicans were not going to make the difference in 2008's tight race. So I came to a decision. Moving to Ohio was out (I could never leave the woman who cuts my hair, or my family), but for the good of my party, on the fifteenth day of September before the fourth day of November, I went to Town Hall and changed my registration. Just like that—*zip*—I severed my Democratic roots and joined that elite, most-sought-after group of election makers, known simply as the Independents.

The way I figured it, as soon as this took place, I would no longer be a party grunt, whose vote does not have to be won or even gotten out. I would now be in the happy position of being wooed by Republicans and Democrats alike, because they knew my vote could go either way. That's what a "swing" vote is. It's the kind that tips elections; it's the unpredictable pull of the lever that shoots one candidate over the top. It's the important one.

My reason for switching was twofold. First, I did it for

my party, because I was joining the group they were working hardest to win. The second reason was a little more personal. To tell the truth, I'd always wondered what it would feel like to be an INDEPENDENT, just floating out there, unaffiliated, uncommitted, unknown to the Democratic National Committee. It's true, in my state I now would not be able to vote in a primary, and I might miss those personal My-Fellow-Democrat letters from Hillary Clinton, James Carville, or Ted Kennedy, but I was cool with that. I was beginning to feel they didn't really know me anyway, or they would have remembered I always checked "other" in the contribution box.

I also knew that Republicans would try to have their way with me. Not a bad thing. I've had dance partners before I didn't go home with, and one can still learn a lot from the experience. Although I don't want to glorify my role as enemy informant, my new position, Independent-at-large, probably gave a little more import to my frequent communications with Howard Dean. This is not just another Democrat writing, Howard. An INDEPENDENT knows something you may want to hear. And if *you* don't, maybe Mike Duncan *will*.

I might not even have had to write any more letters. In my new role as kingmaker, I expected to be polled frequently. (INDEPENDENTS usually are.) And just to add a little suspense to the mix, and to keep the courtship going, when asked for whom I was going to vote, I planned to answer, "I'm undecided"; that way, I was a real wild card, both INDEPENDENT and undecided. Even Ralph Nader would have thought he had a chance.

I only went through the change for a few short months before the election, so I can't say I knew any other INDEPENDENTS personally, but I planned to look around to see if there was any place we Indies hung out. I didn't find any, probably because it doesn't make any sense that a whole bunch of free thinkers would all be heading to the same Starbucks. No matter. The polls showed me to be one of a growing group, which is more than they ever said for me when I was a Democrat.

And as we approached the big election in the fall I felt confident—at last, my much-sought-after vote would really count. Because *they* knew and *I* knew, it ain't over 'til the fat lady swings.

Post-Party Blues

I know what's going to happen. I've been through these elections before. On the Monday before the Tuesday of Election Day, my mailbox will be stuffed with cards and flyers asking me to support this or that candidate. The phone will ring all day with callers telling me where my voting place is and reminding me, incidentally, to vote for X, Y, or Z. I'll hear from my good friends in high places: Bill Clinton, Steven Spielberg, George Clooney, Caroline Kennedy Schlossberg. "Dear Lyla"—we're on a first-name basis now, mine.

Then suddenly, it will be the Wednesday after the Tuesday of Election Day. And wham, bam, thank you, ma'am—the courtship is over. No more how-are-you-todays from my friends at party headquarters. Jim Himes, Christopher Shays, Toni Boucher will have conveniently forgotten where I live.

Never mind that I attended rallies all over the state, wrote Letters to the Editors; paid more to have coffee with Hillary Clinton than I do in Starbucks (and it wasn't even a latte). For months they stressed how much we had in common, how they knew I shared their views on transportation, gun control, the war in Iraq, tax cuts, health care—I thought we were in a relationship.

At the very least, we were pen pals. They sent me letters, I sent them money. Not a lot of money. I mostly checked "other." But they assured me they would appreciate anything I could give. Ha!

Then, on Election Night, I follow my usual routine. The returns come in. I go to bed and wake up in the morning to silence: It's over. My only mail is a note from The Candidate sent with a nonprofit stamp three weeks before. A brief look at the newspaper indicates most of my candidates have lost, which means, contrary to what I was told, my contribution *didn't* make the difference between winning and losing after all.

It's Black Wednesday, that's for sure. I don't know how the country will stumble along with all the wrong people in office. But I will probably deal with my political hangover just as I have every other year. First, I'll try to scrape the bumper stickers off of my car. Then I'll put my campaign buttons into my "Political Mementos" box, along with pictures, flyers, and a few of those "personal" letters. Then on the afternoon of the day after the election, misty-eyed, I'll get out the flour, get out the butter, and let my tears moisten the dough as I roll out my pies for Thanksgiving.

The Rewards Program

Please, no more self-addressed labels with pictures of adorable kittens or tiny beagles, ears flopping almost to label's edge. And don't try to tempt me with your calendars: magnificent close-ups of tigers or lions greeting me as I turn from January to February or March to April. No matter what you send me (although I wouldn't completely reject the idea of a new car), I'm only going to contribute to your cause once a year, and then only if you're a cause I believe in. What's more, if you want my help in preserving a species I not only didn't know was endangered but in fact didn't even know existed before I got your mailing, you'll have to wait your turn. As far as saving the bearded catfish of Qatar, I know I've never eaten this particular species, so I've already done my part. While I don't doubt there is a threat of annihilation, I don't feel as guilty as I would if I were out hunting leopard.

That's not to say I'm unwilling to do my share. I understand the need for fund-raising, I've done a bit of it myself. But when I do donate to a worthy cause, I would like to see my money go to that worthy cause, not to the purchase of labels or calendars or mugs or note cards or T-shirts or key rings or photo albums or pens or a shiny new nickel. Save your money for the kids, the whales, the polar bears, the rhinoceroses, the cats, the dogs, the orchids, the monuments, my alma mater, my husband's alma mater, victims of hurricanes, tsunamis, earthquakes, typhoons, mudslides, brush fires, hunger, war, poverty, to name a few. No one is going to contribute to a cause for a new key ring. And if, as in my case, you put your house key and your mini plastic cards for Borders, CVS, YMCA, Stop & Shop, Food Emporium, Barnes and Noble on the key ring that came with your car, another one or two or three or four to remind you that you donated to the end-of-the-world foundation only means you have to make another decision as to what can or cannot be recycled.

I feel particularly put-upon when, not a week after I have sent $5, $10, $25, or "other" to a seemingly worthwhile cause, I receive The Letter.

Dear Lyla Blake Ward,

The mammals of North America thank you for your generous gift. It is people like you, who have consistently stood against the use of whale oil for your lamps and have not let blubber into your lives, who are responsible for the large number of humpbacks still actively gobbling up the lesser fish life of the Atlantic.

In fact, we are so grateful for your recent gift, we would now like to ask if you would contribute to our continuing effort again this week. For your convenience, we have enclosed a self-addressed stamped envelope, which we hope you won't use, because, by affixing your own first-class stamp instead, you will increase the value of your gift.

Thank you.

Your Friends at NAHO

North American Humpback Organization

Deal. I won't use your prestamped envelope if you won't send me any more labels. And in the end, we both know that will mean fewer Dumpsters for fewer humpsters.

It's Only a Paper Boon

On the upside, I think I now have a handle on what derivatives are. On the downside, my life's savings are worth half of what they were before I began the learning process.

But not to worry. According to the financial analysts whose ranks have grown faster than the national debt, as long as I don't sell, it's only a paper loss. Sounds reasonable except that when I bought the stock I paid real money, or as close to real money as a check gets. So who has my money now? Was it shredded? Is it on somebody else's paper? All I know is: in years past when my stocks and bonds were showing a *gain*, also only on paper, I felt a whole lot better. Did someone else feel a whole lot worse?

I'd be the first to admit, my knowledge of higher finance does not run deep (wouldn't I gladly trade that semester of Medieval Poetry for a course on Economics); but I do know I'd have to be living in a cave not to understand that, paper-shmaper, a loss is a loss is a loss.

Besides, it is my earnest belief that paper and its coconspirator, plastic (along with 24/7 news channels, but that's for another essay), have gotten us into the mess we're in now. Instead of gold backing up paper, we have paper backing up paper. I'm not suggesting we go back on the gold standard; no one knows for sure how much gold there is left in them thar hills, but the old days, when a housewife could break off a piece of bullion and take it to the store to buy a new bonnet, and we could tell how rich someone was just by counting his bricks, are looking pretty good right now.

Wishful thinking aside, I'm convinced the only greenbacks in circulation are the $20 bills in ATM machines and the assorted change in the tellers' drawers at the bank. How can we be sure the big money we were allowed to see when the Federal Reserve opened its vaults to the TV-viewing public is real? On *Without a Trace*, when the ransom money is paid, usually only the top bills are legitimate—the rest are phonies. I don't know anyone, personally, who has held a million dollars unstacked in her hands recently. In fact, now that I think of it, I've been invited to go on many house tours, kitchen tours, garden tours, but I don't remember the last time anyone asked me if I wanted to go on a tour of my bank's vault to see my money.

Looking back, it's amazing how many transactions take place without so much as a dollar bill making an appearance. My Social Security check is deposited directly into my checking account, and the other income I receive is also paid by check, supposedly against funds in the issuers' respective banks. On my end, I pay my bills online and the bank pays my bills by check, supposedly drawn against funds in my bank account. When we sold our house and bought another, no one came to the table with a wad of bills. We wrote a check, the buyers wrote a check, the bank wrote a check; not one of us saw the actual money the checks were drawn against.

So looking at my desk with its mountains of stock certificates, credit card receipts, canceled checks, and other stand-ins for actual cash, I have to feel cheered. Assuming those youngsters who are running the world now are right, and paper represents actual money, I don't care if the Dow moves up, down, or sideways, anyone looking at my stacks would have to say, there goes one well-endowed lady.

Just Rewards

The state of the economy, mine in particular, has caused me to take stock (not *stock* stock, but a reckoning of my possessions). And I've been pleased to find out that my saving ways of the past, so derided in the family, may allow me to continue my lifelong habits of health and cleanliness despite the rising costs of those products necessary to keep me from any premature withering. Without getting too specific, let's just say I have enough darling little bars of soap, tiny bottles of shampoo (some with conditioner), body lotion, and shower caps, garnered from my travels, to last me, and any visitors, for the rest of our natural lives.

And it's a good thing, too, because hotels are obviously not thinking of contestants on *The Biggest Loser* when they order their courtesy baskets, so one can squeeze only two or possibly three shampoos from the half-ounce bottle given by even the most generous hostelries. The same goes for the mini body lotions that are used up in direct relation to the size of your body. One person's torso is another person's toe. Whereas soap, even finger-sized, can last for several washings, unless you take an unusually long shower or, like my husband, insist on using two at a time. Luckily, the shower caps given in little boxes, though a trifle delicate, are one size fits all. I don't use shower caps, myself, but I have an impressive collection just the same, because you never know when someone who *does* use one may stop by to take a shower.

The generosity of hotels doesn't stop with toiletries. I have saved enough squares of chocolate left on my pillow to throw even a healthy person into a diabetic coma. I have to confess, it didn't take a recession for me to arrange the various "hotels" on a plate and serve them as after-dinner mints. I consider these delicious mementos worldly. My kids say they're tacky.

Thinking back on my travels, any money spent on airfare, for instance, has come back to me in the form of tangible rewards that cannot be trivialized in times like these. It's no secret that flying Business Class does cost a trifle more than flying Coach, but the savings are a lot like taking home a doggie bag after an expensive restaurant meal. You pay $26 for the restaurant steak, which is huge, so you take half home for "the doggie." In reality, you have the other half for lunch the next day, which means dinner cost $13, and lunch the next day is free. (Remember the bulldog incident in *Life With Father*?)

Translating that into Business Class perks, how can you put a price on earplugs, an eye mask, folding slippers, a teeny-tiny tube of toothpaste, an undersized toothbrush, perfect for a few prominent front teeth (if you try putting it any farther back, you'll swallow it), all tidily arranged in a stunning navy or black waterproof kit, which, if it were not for the airline letters emblazoned in Arabic, Cyrillic, or Hindi on the front, could easily be mistaken for a Gucci bag.

Wait. I don't think I mentioned the sewing kits offered by both hotels and airlines, if you fly luxury class. Over the years, I have cornered the market on these darling little kits that have not only black and white thread but sometimes even a color that matches the torn garment I'm trying to repair. In the plummy days of bull markets, I'll admit, I was not sure why I had kept all these tiny lengths of thread, but now that the bears have taken over, I give thanks every time I don't have to dip into my reserves to stitch up a fallen hem. And with a powerful magnifying glass, I can even find the eye of the needle.

One of the things that worries me most about these economic hard times is how badly prepared the younger generations are for adjusting to a less profligate way of life. When they can't squeeze that last inch of toothpaste out of the tube, they throw it away. Done. Finished. Buy a new one. Do you know how many shampoos I've gotten out of a bottle my visiting daughters considered empty?

Bear or bull, I feel confident I can survive the market swings. I can go to my closet, drawer, or storage bin and find hundreds of creams, lotions, and detergents, albeit in dwarf-size containers. *I* don't have to go to the store. But I'm not so sure about *my* children and *their* children. In all honesty, they don't have their mother's assets, either because, one, they never took the generous gifts offered by the hotel or airplane or even ladies' rooms in fine restaurants; or two, without a thought to the future, they defiantly used both the hand bar and the bath bar during their overnight stay at the Marriott.

Now, as they watch their 401k's reduced to 201k's, there's only one answer for them. They have to mend their ways, and my major concern is: where are they going to find the thread?